GOD'S BOOT CAMP

Araceli Ganan Almond, MD (2017)

Araceli Ganan Almond, MD
as told to
Greenbrier Almond, MD

Greenbrier Almond MD

(2017)

International Standard Book Number 0-87012-880-9
Library of Congress Control Number 2017914413
Printed in the United States of America
Copyright © 2017 by Araceli Ganan Almond, MD
Buckhannon, WV

2017

McClain Printing Company
Parsons, WV
www.mcclainprinting.com
2017

*Front cover art by
Bob and Tyler McMahon*

Illustrations by Tyler McMahon

DEDICATION

Dedicated to God, Who inspired my practice of medicine to relieve suffering and show compassion like Jesus, the Great Physician. Trusting God's leading through the Holy Spirit, I came to America. Then when I resisted writing a memoir, God graciously supplied His Word through the Prophet Isaiah, commanding me:

> So, go now and write all this down. Put it in a book so that the record will be there to instruct the coming generations.
> —Isaiah 30: 8 (The Message)

ABOUT THE ARTIST

The artwork for this book was proudly created by Tyler McMahon. Tyler is 11 years old and lives in Southern California with her parents and beloved dog, Riley. Tyler is a great student, a Girl Scout, plays percussion in the school band and the ukulele. She loves reading, Minecraft and all things related to dogs.

Her favorite sports are swimming, badminton and running. She loves to go on hikes where she can talk your ears off. She takes advantage of the wonderful Southern California weather and loves to be outside.

You will find her most days reading, finding unusual ways to do the usual, or being with her favorite dog, Riley.

TABLE OF CONTENTS

FOREWORD

Our mother has never been one to settle in the past or rely upon the vagaries of a presumed destiny. Instead we have watched her ever reaching towards the future in order to seize it, propelled by an unshakable faith in God's promise. Many of her early childhood touchstones—from family pictures to her birth certificate—were destroyed before she reached maturity. Born during an era of unrest and occupation in World War II, she had no choice but to seek future hope; facing the uncertainty of an immigrant's life, she was determined to chart her course.

For us children, this meant that portions our mother's life, her past, remained a mystery. When she did share her stories of youth, what we heard about were her childhood dreams—the aspirations of America, a desire to practice medicine and serve others, the prayers for a life partner, her hopes for us. When we began encouraging her to tell more of her life stories, she would balk, suddenly, strangely shy. And then one day she told us coyly, "You'd be surprised if you knew the truth!" Out tumbled these stories of daring, romance, adventure, and danger, all of which strengthened her faith and led her to the comforting serenity of West Virginia's hills. Surprising, indeed.

As children, touches with our mother's immigrant story were mainly felt through her idiosyncrasies, cultural and personal—the rice she cooked with every meal, regardless; the giant carved wooden fork and spoon hung in the kitchen, the gateway to the always overstocked pantry; a strict, unfailing and (often painful) disciplining for infractions of household rules; the tendency to save everything for a potential secondary use (recycling was our fashion long before environmentalism came to Buckhannon); a special emphasis on education and the firm expectation of achievement for her children; spontaneous renditions of the gospel "His Eye Is on the Sparrow," piano chords carrying her sonorous voice through the halls of 48 South Kanawha Street; the stray cat she assiduously shooed away for weeks until eventually relenting and adopting as a favorite; the people for whom she did the same thing; the tendency towards an automatic "no"—a moment of caution—before a full embrace.

Our mother has approached life with a studied prudence that hangs in balance with a great spirit of openness and adventure. And because of our mother, our life has never been short on adventure.

As very young children we visited our mother's homeland. There are blurred memories of the white sand beaches of the Visayan Islands we explored as pre-schoolers (family myth has it that Ronce once cried out "Snow, Mommy!" on seeing one pristine stretch of sand); and the rickety, overcrowded ferry that brought us there, crammed with large rooms of bunk beds and a steerage brimming with hammocks and floor mats, all full of staring eyes and the lilting tones of the local dialect. We even attended school in Odiongan for several months, ferried daily by pedal rickshaw from the family home where the Ganan name was forged into the metalwork of the fence on which the local children would bang daily after school, crying out to us to join them. Our experiences in the Philippines taught us about customs and culture, but they also exposed us to what it felt like to be a semi-outsider. Like us in our mother's land, our Filipina mother in Appalachia is someone who looks different, speaks differently, yet has roots buried below the surface that anchor her there as strongly and proudly as any other Mountaineer.

Our mother's unassuming, unvarnished stories expose those roots—bonds that extend across oceans, rise up mountains, and remind us of her tenacity and strength during times of adversity, when she was forced to confront questions of her identity, intellect, and faith. She recognized early, even innately, that God's path for her was to be long and challenging. As Micah explained, what does the Lord require of you? To act justly and to love mercy and to walk humbly with your God. She carried forward in this manner, determined to realize God's promise.

Our mother—a brave adventurer, who was the first in her family to immigrate, a female physician, who broke through walls of bias, a pioneering minority in Appalachia, who challenged conventions of race and love, a devoted Christian, who followed her faith despite the consequences—never cowered to fear, even when the threats loomed most ominously. In this book she continues to follow that courageous path—candidly opening her life up for review and examination. For us, it is an inspiration.

Maria Luisa Ganan Almond
Roncevert David Ganan Almond

ACKNOWLEDGMENTS

Like my beloved father-in-law, a wonderful physician, acknowledged in his memoir book, I especially "wish to thank my medical colleagues, my nursing staff, and my patients, who blessed me with a long and satisfying practice."

A special thanks to my family for their enthusiasm and help. To my husband, Greenbrier, for always asking questions and carefully listening to my stories. He is an excellent writer, so his suggestions improved the text. To my daughter, Maria, thanks for the hugs and shared tears at discouraging times while encouraging me to keep telling my story from start to finish. To my son, Roncevert, thanks for enlarging my international perspective. My family certainly continues "mighty in the land" as promised in God's Word (Psalm 112:2).

Kimberly Gilmore continues to offer compassionate, competent, and Christian editing. She has helped Greenbrier on four other books and all the Almond Children together for their *Stories of a West Virginia Family*.

The Reverend Doctor Gary Mallonee listened as an American Veteran and a Minister of the Gospel to the whole story. Thanks indeed, Gary. The concept of God's Boot Camp might have been impossible to actualize without your patient listening to my life story of ever-increasing faith.

I want to honor my parents, who placed balanced emphasis on a life of Christian Faith and Service as well as striving academic performance through medical school in the Philippines. My siblings lived much of my Filipino "Coming-to-America" story with me, sharing my surprise at what God has done. I thank my family profusely.

PREFACE

Memoir writing never has been high on my "to do" list. I feel so inadequate as an author and am embarrassed to expose my life to the world. However, I have had important people in my life urge me to write my story. My dear husband Greenbrier has encouraged it from the day he was inspired to write following our daughter Maria's announcement of her pregnancy. We want our grandchildren to know our lives and our lessons learned.

My first directive came from my pediatric training director, Herbert Pomerance, MD. His wife became my cheerleader with good telephone support for my impending thyroid surgery in February 1975. A month later, after I recovered from my surgery and was back to pediatric residency training, Dr. Pomerance came to my table while I was eating lunch alone in our cafeteria. He stood by my table, looked around, looked at me and said, "It is amazing! Write everything down!" and took off. I was puzzled and pondered a lot about it for awhile, but life went on.

"I will not tell my life story in a book unless God will tell me to," I exclaimed to Greenbrier in March 2015 after we returned from our trip to the Holy Land. I just blurted that out to stop him from asking me to do it! Well, three days later God finally got my attention. I came to our breakfast table after Greenbrier had finished eating food while feasting on God's Word during his Bible study. As I prepared to break my overnight fast, my eyes fell on the Bible opened to Isaiah 30.

Wow! There as a directive from God I read:

> So, go now and write all this down.
>   Put it in a book
> So that the record will be there
>   to instruct the coming generations,
> Because this is a rebel generation,

a people who lie,
A people unwilling to listen
  to anything God tells them.
They tell their spiritual leaders,
  "Don't bother us with irrelevancies."
They tell their preachers,
  "Don't waste our time on impracticalities.
Tell us what makes us feel better.
Don't bore us with obsolete religion.
That stuff means nothing to us.
  Quit hounding us with The Holy of Israel.
            —Isaiah 30: 8-11 (The Message)

"Write all this down. Put it in a book"! My eyes got big. The verses spoke to my heart and soul. The reason I had to do this book about my life was obedience. I felt God was telling me what He wanted me to do, so I had to obey.

I only wanted to write the real happenings, no sugar-coating, no exaggerations. I set out to tell my story the way it happened as I remember it. It seems that my life is not real, but it is! And God has been with me all along. Initially I thought my book would be called *The Golden Cage*, but the title *God's Boot Camp* came shortly after through the inspiration of the Holy Spirit.

Correctly discerning my path, Greenbrier called his lifelong friend, who has military service as well as a doctorate in theology, to assist. The Reverend Dr. Gary L. Mallonee listened to my story in its entirety. With his life experience and education as well as love of our Lord and Savior Jesus Christ, he has helped me tell an amazing true story of coming to America, seeking a deeper walk with Jesus, both losing and gaining freedom in the living of my days.

Now, may you the reader gain from my telling you my story. "And ye shall know the truth, and the truth shall make you free." (John 8:32 KJV)

INTRODUCTION

LEANING ON THE EVERLASTING ARMS

The Greyhound bus from Atlanta, Georgia, climbed ever upward into the Appalachian Mountains. My eyes filled with wonder at the beauty of America. I felt God's embrace as I hummed the song:

> Leaning, leaning,
> Safe and secure from all alarms;
> Leaning, leaning,
> Leaning on the everlasting arms.

Soon I would join my sister Bella in Dallas, Texas. No job. Little money. But trusting in God, surrounded by His goodness, I felt safe and secure.

On our way, the bus driver stopped at a rest area. I debarked the bus, excited to experience my first hail storm. Tiny drops of ice from the sky! How very thrilled I was! A male passenger in the bus shared the moment, telling me about the Smoky Mountains.

I prayed for a chance to return some day, God willing. My heart sang, "I was poorly born on the top of the mountain," a Filipino folk song capturing the mood of the storm. What a country! Growing up on a small island makes one dream of other places. I had dreamed of the USA. Now my dreams were coming true.

Events unknown to me at the moment of this mountaintop experience would seem to go against such dreams. I would find myself facing challenges down the road that seemed hard to imagine. Like a childhood game of hide and seek, America—land of the free and home of the brave and of opportunity—opened up before me.

Yes, I testify, God has been with me all along. I feel His Presence even now. I was young and full of hope and faith in God and myself about tomorrow. Now in my retirement years, I continue to thank God for my life and blessings. I have two wonderful children and four granddaughters, a husband who loves me, and the promise that "greater is He that is in me than he that is in this world"! (I John 4:4) I recite this verse daily in my walking exercises, as well as "I can do all things through Christ which strengtheneth me." (Philippians 4:13)

My God is full of grace, faithful and real! Praise the Lord!

BLESSED BEGINNINGS: LIFE IN THE PHILIPPINES

MY EARLY LIGHT SHINES

Perhaps some casual observer of Greenbrier and me would wonder about a match-up of a rare Polynesian orchid and a West Virginia wildflower. As Greenbrier ponders: "What influences on Araceli allowed her to eye a West Virginia Mountaineer, string-bean thin, hair too long, and beard unruly? Quite an improbable pairing to be sure. Certainly Araceli let me know from the beginning that she came from an outstanding family and a wonderful country. Furthermore, she came to America trusting God explicitly to direct her steps. She sought God's best."

My "once upon a time" story began with my birth on the small island of Tablas, Romblon Province, Visayan region, Philippine Islands on June 17, 1942, in the midst of World War II.

Tablas Island, isolated in the vast Pacific Ocean, became populated by four people groups exploring Polynesia. Local fiestas celebrate those brave souls who explored from four directions, each with their own language. Then for 400 years, Tablas Island supplied the finest wood in the far-flung Spanish empire. The word *tablas* means "plank." From the trees came the raw timber for Spanish ships. In these same deep forests during World War II, my mother and siblings and I evacuated away from the Japanese during an extended occupation. Food was scarce, so she nursed longer than most.

I am the middle of nine children, being the sixth child from the oldest. Mom gave birth about every two years. One sister died in infancy.

I laugh, "I'm old but wise! Are you surprised?"

At that time of my birth, my father was the mayor of Despujols, our little town during the Japanese Occupation. (The name was later changed to San Andres, in honor of Saint Andrew.) Father had to deal with the Japanese in a very civil way to save the people and our family from

2

persecution. You heard about the babies being tossed into the air and stuck through by the bayonets. I don't think it was on my island, but you heard the stories. Of course, I was born during that time, I was just a baby. I don't remember these things; I only heard stories.

My father became a hero for the little town because he actually dealt with the Japanese and made a lot of deals that we had to provide this, provide that, as the Japanese demanded. My father talked to the powerful people in town, too. He kept us all safe by his ability to negotiate.

We Filipinos love to sing. There is a ballad in honor of my father. In fact, the old folks sang it to us as children. Now my hope is that somebody is still alive who will teach me the ballad's lyrics and melody.

Anyway, I grew up on that small island only about 10 miles across and 30 miles long. My father was very much a disciplinarian to the eight young Ganans. Later in life when we saw the movie *The Sound of Music*, he recognized he had fallen into the same trap as Captain Von Trapp. Then he mellowed.

He was initially part of the independent Catholic religion because Filipinos are mainly Catholic. We had 400 years with the Spaniard Colonization. They prescribed our religion and language. My father used to speak Spanish in court. He was a judge too, later on. But he was mayor for two terms of the town, including during the Japanese time. Then he became a circuit judge.

An early decision of my parents was to embrace Protestant Christianity, which put us in a minority role. My father became a Protestant during his imprisonment for three months on another island. All mayors were imprisoned at that time, during the war. Anyway, my mother thought my father would never make it back. Then one night he came back home. I think I remember barely when my father came home, but I don't remember many things of that time.

3

There were so many of us, and our father had to be very strict with us. But adopting a Holiness doctrine of the Christian faith made him more strict. We were not allowed to wear fancy jewelry or to wear makeup. (Sometimes when he was gone during the week and coming home for the weekend, we would have to scramble to find something to scrape off the nail polish from our nails so he wouldn't see it. Otherwise, our hands would be smacked with a ruler!) We were not allowed to dance, because dancing could be too intimate. We were not allowed to go to big parties. We were very conservative. That is the way we were brought up. We could not even go to town fiestas, because the meaning of fiesta was to honor the saints, and we were Protestants.

A Filipino man named Diaz was an itinerant pastor who went to the United States to join the Navy and served maybe 15, 20 years, and then came back to the Philippines with a burning desire to witness to the people. He witnessed to my family. First my uncle converted and then all the Ganans became Fundamental Christians.

At first my father, being a politician, went to church, but it was not influencing his daily walk very much. Then he became very Christian when he was imprisoned during the war. In fact, his favorite song was "What a Friend We Have in Jesus."

ROBIN HOOD, MY FATHER'S HERO

Br'er Rabbit stories in Appalachia, told as bedtime stories by Greenbrier's father, had a counterpoint in the Philippines, where my father told us Robin Hood stories. All the children gathered around for story time. Father would sit in a rocking chair and we would sit around him, and he would tell us the Robin Hood story.

Robin Hood was an heroic outlaw in English folklore who, according to legend, was a highly skilled archer and swordsman. He is often portrayed as "robbing from the rich and giving to the poor" alongside his band of Merry Men. Robin Hood became a popular folk figure in the late-medieval period. That the Robin Hood mythology traveled around the world to remote South Pacific Islands is quite remarkable.

He was my father's hero. That's why my father always liked to help the poor. He was a lawyer and he helped the poor a lot. In fact, he said, "If people come to the house and knock on the door, and they have no shoes, are poorly clothed, invite them in and feed them. They are usually hungry. They don't have food, so feed them. That's an order." So we were brought up that way; we were partial to the poor.

There was a minority group in Mindoro called *Mangyan* that just wore g-strings. One person named Pudit from that minority group stayed with us. He amused the town folks by climbing up coconut trees upside-down, his feet first. My father was helping him because someone was taking his land from him. Minority people were not educated people. My father took Pudit to Manila. He gave him clothes, because you could not go into the city with just g-strings. People would stare at you.

Since our family accepted Jesus as our Lord and Savior, we prayed for the Gospel outreach to the *Mangyan*. When I was just a child, most of them did not really believe in God, but now some have become Christian.

On telling his tales, my father expanded on the protection afforded by Sherwood Forest. We had wonderful tropical rainforests, so my imagination ran wild about a vast Sherwood Forest. In 2002 our son Ronce actually visited Sherwood Forest. My father would have been so pleased.

WISE LIKE SOLOMON

Mixed messages from my childhood led me to a moment of prayer when I was in the fourth or fifth grade. I thought about it a lot. I prayed as a child to God, "I want to be wise like Solomon." I reasoned that he did not ask for money or wealth, but he asked for wisdom. I said I wanted to be wise like him. If you are very wise you will be very rich anyway! Yes, I laugh now, but I remember that very well.

God gave me a measure of wisdom. This helped me understand what was happening in our family and community. For example, we were taught by our Sunday School teachers that as Protestant Christians, we were not to go to the town fiesta, because the festival was to honor the saints.

What I figured out wisely is that my purpose is to honor God daily by loving God and loving neighbor. That way I can keep all the commandments.

Just to show that I was not a perfect child, I want the granddaughters to know that one day my parents left us to take a short trip. All of us were entrusted to two mature, single women in our church. These ladies were sisters. My father was circuit judge and my mother was a fourth-grade teacher. Maybe she wasn't in school at that time. Probably the time frame was Friday, Saturday and Sunday.

On Sunday our church had an outreach out to the barrios. The two spinsters wanted to go, but we were under their care. However, my siblings and I didn't want to go. Actually, we were conniving with our cousins, who came down from another island, to see the movie called *Now and Forever*. It was a true story involving the first-ever Miss Universe, Armi Helena Kuusela from Finland. In real life she had a romantic episode with one of our local businessmen, and they got married eventually. The movie was their love story. We were interested. It was very popular in the Philippines.

I don't know where we got the money, but after our lady caretakers left for the church function, we went to the movie. We had convinced these gullible ladies that our parents had people who could help us at home. Our servants would take good care of us while they were away, we had told them.

My, my! The movie house was just across the street. We knew better. The only movie our father would allow at that time was *Tarzan*. Certainly a spicy love story was verboten.

We snuck out of the house and went to see the movie. In my spirit I knew God was watching over us. A tropical thunderstorm blew up. The theatre was shaking with a thrashing downpour of rain and the stormy blasts of lightning and thunder. Feeling God was judging us, we became frightened. We looked at each other. Without staying for the movie, we left the theatre in a panic, running across the now-muddy street, getting soaked by the rain. We arrived home safely but without an alibi.

How we prayed to God, asking for forgiveness on our knees with tears in our eyes. Our cousins who were visiting were not spared from interrogation and spanking. My father used his leather belt and gave us two whippings each. Edna, the youngest, came late with bulging buttocks from pillows she had put under her pants to soften the blows! We all giggled quietly from our seats. I suspect even my father was secretly amused by her ingenuity!

MOTHER

Mother and I shared a special bond from our extended time of nursing at the height of World War II when I was born June 17, 1942. Then there was my asthma from the third grade on with the privilege and attention of being in the sick role—I was privileged to ask for orange soda, which was then a treat to have. Even when she was my teacher in the fourth grade, our teacher/student role proved very tight. I am not saying that I was as smart as my mother, but I did identify with her and wanted to follow her career path.

My mother, Maria Villanueva Ganan, was my teacher when I was in fourth grade, section 1. The school was divided into sections by grades. We *A* students had to be in her class—section 1. I definitely could not be a *B* or *C* student. I could not be in a lower section, as I was smart enough to belong to section 1. My how very strict she was with me. I felt that Mother was more strict with me than my classmates, maybe to show no favoritism.

Teaching perhaps would not have been my mother's choice, given her druthers. In that period of time, a woman either became a nurse or a teacher. She chose to become a teacher and went to the Philippine Normal College. She became one of the best teachers in her district.

During my time, women can choose to study what they want to like men. Thank You, God!

ONLY BELIEVE

By 14 years of age, my relationship with God had grown by leaps and bounds. Our family life centered around our church life. Maybe not required as an article of faith, but due to custom I went to the front many times to receive Jesus Christ as Lord and Savior. In Charismatic worship, or maybe as a mass hysteria thing, or whatever, I went often to the altar for prayer.

My faith grew for sure. When I was in fifth grade, my sisters and I were playing on the monkey bars after school. I was balancing on top, and one of my sisters pulled me down. I fell on my back. I was not able to breathe, I was gasping for breath. My sisters ran off, so I was left alone there. The only thing I could do was to say, "God." When I was able to utter the name "God," I was able to breathe. God heard my cry, answered my prayer and sustained me.

For some time I was having backache, but I never told my family about it. I never told my mother because my sister would get in trouble. So at night I would put a Bible under my back, because at that time I already believed in healing. I would lie down on it, hoping God would heal me. Hallelujah, He did.

After a few weeks, I got better. I was able to sleep without pain. To God be the glory, I had the Bible on my back every night. And my sisters knew that, too. Things like that happened in fifth grade. I was already God-fearing at that time. I tell the story not to shame my siblings but to honor God.

Another sign of my growing faith is this: One day during summertime, we children wanted to steal from the school garden across the fence from our home. The temptation of satisfying hunger was real. On the weekend there was nobody there. So my sisters and I said we wanted to get corn, to steal the corn from the garden. It was right across our fence. We went over.

Actually I was already going to pluck the corn, and then I remembered:

> Be careful little eyes what you see.
> Be careful little feet where you go.
> Be careful little hands what you do!

That Christian Sunday School song stopped me in my tracks right then and there. I resisted temptation and climbed back over the fence to our yard.

Those songs you learn in church are very powerful, very, very powerful. They ministered to me. Later I shared songs, ministering to others. The Word turned me around.

Amazing grace, I was 14 years old, growing in faith. My active mind questioned: "They say God is all-powerful, all-present, all-knowledgeable. Wow. If it's true what they're telling us in Church, in Bible school, in Sunday school, about this Christ who died for us, then I have two choices: believe completely or not believe at all."

So at that time I said, "God, if You are all-knowing, all-present, You know what I'm thinking right now. I'm questioning You, if it's true or not. I have a choice—to believe You or not believe You." I reasoned to myself, "If I choose not to believe, I lose everything, I go to hell. That's what it said. But if I believe, I have everything to gain. Supposing it's not true and I believe, I still gain, nothing will happen. But if I don't believe and if it's true, then I lose everything." I didn't want to lose. I am not a loser.

So I said, "God, I want to believe." And I did and still do, much more now. I think that's the time I really actually became a Christian, because I was really knowing. I had been to the front altar many times before, I wasn't giving up. But this time I was doing it on my own.

HEALING MIRACLES

Aline and Jack Richey, newly married American missionaries, came to Tablas Island in 1949. They joined our church, which was called a Full Gospel Center, being an independent, very conservative church at that time. Through their influence we became part of the Four Square Gospel Church. Healing miracles, part of the Charismatic Christian doctrine, took on a great emphasis.

As a child I did not know much about it, but I knew that our church split. Some members left to continue Holiness practices. But my father decided to stay with the American missionaries. He was fluent in many languages and dialects, so he often interpreted for the church services.

Not only did we believe in miracles, but we also knew of Jesus' Second Coming. He is coming back, though we don't know when. My father said we must be active in loving God and neighbor. He was mayor and then judge, so we were well off financially. Moreover, in the community the Ganans were highly esteemed and well respected.

My curiosity for spiritual matters included wanting to see an angel and to experience a miracle. The supernatural phenomenon of Jesus' life was real. Why could I not say, "God, I want to see an angel"? The angel appeared to Mary, right? Nowadays, I reasoned, an angel could appear to a Philippine Island girl. Sometimes I would pray on a group excursion to the beach. I would pray, looking up to the massive cumulus clouds, that I might see Jesus or an angel.

My longing for supernatural healing took a serious turn when I developed allergic asthma in the third grade after a trip to Manila. Short of breath, I would sit up and argue with God just like I knew my father would argue a case before a judge as an attorney. "If I am going to be growing up like this, with asthma, with this allergy, smite me now. I would rather be dead. Take me home now."

Fortunately by the time I was in high school, my

asthma disappeared. I was happy with that, that God healed me. When I was praying, I would always pray at night, grateful for healthy breathing. Then as sleep came, I would dream about the Second Coming. I would wonder morning, noon or night: When will Christ come? Certainly, my hope and dream would be that Christ might come in my lifetime.

Then something happened that strengthened my faith greatly. We had an epidemic in our town. All the chickens and all the ducks died. There was no veterinary doctor to treat the disease. What a tragedy!

My father taught us to take care of animals. He was a very strong disciplinarian. Animal husbandry definitely was an emphasis. So we had ducks and chickens. Now they were dying or already dead. During lunch break one day, I came home from school. I ran to the coop to see that all the poultry died but my one duck. But his eyes were full of dirt already, he was just lying there dying.

With a measure of childlike faith, I bent down and cleaned the eyes. I was full of compassion because it was my pet dying. Sadly I knew the duck would die no matter what I did. But because I was feeling sorry for the duck, I put clean and dry paper under it. Then I placed drops of water from my fingertips down the throat. My, my. Already twisted contortions of spastic death had overcome my duck. Finally I prayed to God a child's prayer: "We are sinful people, and You heal us, You forgive us. The duck doesn't sin at all. It has no sin. Why don't You heal this duck?" Then I left for afternoon school classes.

Again I paused at the gate to say, "Please God, heal my duck!" That afternoon, about 5:00, I went straight to the coop, thinking my duck would be dead by now. I couldn't find the duck. I said, "Where's the duck?" So I went around and looked. You know where I saw the duck? It was swimming in the pond, alive and well.

Hallelujah! I was so excited. That was the first miracle that I ever experienced. Since then I have seen other

13

miracles, but this miracle blessed my heart so much. Mother shared my joy. My older sisters and brother were in college at that time. But I shared with Edna, Bella and Ned, too. I hope someone remembers this incident.

My belief grew by bounds. I prayed for other healing. One time my father was away. My mother was a teacher, and she was sick. She had a headache. I prayed for my mom. She got well, too. I chose to believe God, saying, "I don't know what tomorrow brings for me, but I believe You. I believe You completely."

From the miracle of my duck being healed, I even prayed for my life partner, a husband for me. I wanted him to be a Christian, same as I was or better. I was very conservative, never having a Filipino boyfriend in my life. By faith I believed God to make the match. However, I did a lot of day-dreaming anyway.

HIGHER EDUCATION

All of the Ganan children studied after high school in Manila. What an expense for our parents, as there was no college loan program. Though not rich, my father was able to mortgage property. Our older brother, Jun, forced the issue with our father, who considered following Filipino custom by educating the males first and the females only as family finances allowed.

Though Jun was ambitious, he said, "If my sisters cannot study, then I stop studying too." Our parents felt compelled for us to study in Manila. Lily, Jesusa, Precy and I matriculated at Philippine Women's University. Edna, still in high school, went to Philippine Christian College for high school in Manila because it was a short walking distance to our apartment. My parents rented an apartment for our common residence, as it was much cheaper than dormitory charges for all of us. We had a maid helping us with the chores, which we could have done for ourselves. However, household help is very common in the Philippines for those who are able to afford it. Bella and Ned stayed with my parents, who at that time moved to the island of Mindoro.

Student life agreed with my natural bent and ability. Uniformly I did well academically. Again my brother Jun observed: "You get very good grades in the sciences." Indeed, I topped the class. Even in high school where I didn't study enough and wasn't disciplined enough, I was bright enough to be in the top ten. So my brother said, "Why don't you become a doctor like my fiancée?"

Through his influence I became a doctor. Initially I wanted to become a teacher like my mother. She was a very good teacher and an excellent student. She stood out as brilliant. During her time not every woman had the opportunity to go to school. However, she graduated from high school as a valedictorian, earning a scholarship to come to Manila from a small unremarkable northern province. Her life story is quite inspirational.

Higher education actually provided a wonderful interlude in a cocoon, living comfortably. I adapted well from island life to city life. I never had a real problem. I thought to myself: "I am a good person." I was God-fearing, I respected my parents, I honored my parents, and basically I was good. But later on in life I learned that my goodness is nothing in God's eyes. It's all filthy rags. I thought I was really very good. In fact, I prided myself in that. I was proud of myself, that I was a good person, because I didn't fool around, I didn't mess around, lived a clean life, tried not to steal and cheat. These are virtues that are good, but still in God's eyes nothing. I learned that for real later on in God's Boot Camp.

MAKING OF A DOCTOR

Inspiration to pursue medicine instead of teaching came in part from two school classmates. Both studied to be doctors. Tony, whom I admired, was very smart. Like our family, his was Protestant but Baptist. Our mothers were good friends. Also, Benito Male, the elementary principal's son, pursued the healing profession.

The ever-present dichotomy of Protestant versus Catholic came to influence where I studied. I chose not to go to a Catholic school, even a good school like St. Thomas University established during the Spanish time. I didn't want to study the Catechism. Actually, I was very narrow-minded. Rather, I chose the new Far Eastern University Medical School. This is where my classmate Fortunato Elizaga, the fiancée of my older brother and now my sister-in-law, studied. It is a very good, secular private university.

In my second year, a classmate already in the third year named Clarissa P. Carino invited me to go with her to the United States Navy Sangley Point Base Hospital to observe an American physician, Lt. Richard A. Guthrie, who happened to be Mormon. Clarissa's parents were professors at Far Eastern University. By Filipino custom, their daughter needed to have a chaperone to accompany her to the base. Clarissa and I were ripe for a summer experience of medical mentoring by a U.S. Navy Doctor. We made quite a pair, like Mutt and Jeff, as she was short and I was tall by Filipino standard at 5 feet 4 inches. What a privilege to be chosen.

God opened the doors, that I can say. But I don't know why Clarissa selected me, even before we became good friends. She's in the United States now, too. She is retired now, having worked as a successful anesthesiologist in prominent New York City hospitals. Older than I am by maybe two years, she enjoyed a blessed life of sports, including skiing, but never married.

17

How exciting was that summer of 1962. We were given a pass card by Dr. Guthrie to be able to ride in and out of the base by boat in Manila Bay. We rode the hydrofoil, a speed boat for officers from the U.S. Embassy to the naval base located in Cavite. Whoa, what a half-hour ride by hydrofoil speed boat! I was so proud and privileged! Even now, more than 50 years later, I am so excited to describe the honor accorded us.

Later I will tell you, my reader, my dream of being in a mansion looking like the U.S. Supreme Court building with its big pillars. I was dancing with an American guy while all the time looking for Greenbrier, my dear husband. This summer medical externship may be the root of my dream. What a privilege to hobnob with Navy officers.

What a great time we had! All summer, every Friday I would get tokens and put them into the vending machines for chocolates at the base. It was cheap, but more importantly not available in the Philippines. Anyway, I would bring chocolates to my sisters and brothers, who were ecstatic. The Guthries also made me love peanut butter and jelly sandwiches, of which they gave me my first taste. Yummy! I gained some pounds!

All summer we followed Dr. Guthrie around the hospital. One case that's embedded in my mind is a case where they were treating a woman, actually a Filipino woman. She had venereal warts, warts there in her private parts. They were treating her. I think they were putting iodine on and then burning them. I don't know. I was wondering a lot about that, wondering why she had that. Her partner, an American guy, I guess in the Navy, maybe he had them, too. I never saw any other case like that in my life.

Another memorable day on base I was wearing a Navy hat that Dr. Guthrie gave to me as a souvenir. I was very proud of it. But there was a corps man on duty. He didn't like me wearing that hat, and he said, "That's a disgrace to the U.S. Navy." I tell you, I cried. His name was Mr. Smiley. I can't believe I remember the name. I told the lieutenant what he said. That's the last I heard of him or that incident. Otherwise I had a good summer introduction to American medicine, gaining boldness for following my dream to come to the USA.

The Guthries returned to the USA later after our medical experience. They gave me a gift before they left— Handel's *Messiah* recorded by the Mormon Tabernacle Choir. I treasured it. Diane was a nurse by profession but stayed home with her children. I even babysat their two toddlers, Laura and Tammy. Diane and Richard Guthrie were a decent, nice, great American couple. What an outreach to international students! We even had a reunion in Kentucky many, many years later when the good doctor spoke as an expert on diabetes mellitus.

Daily I thank God for Dr. Guthrie's guiding hand in my life that set me on course to be a doctor.

GOLDEN CAGE

"How many millions do you want?" my Chinese suitor asked. He said he could eat me up and put me in his stomach. He said he would put me in a golden cage.

"I don't want a cage, even if it's golden. It's a cage. Who cares if it's gold or not? I don't want to be caged," I declared.

However, he had said, "How many millions do you want?" I thought about that. Wow! I could serve God by building and equipping a Christian medical mission hospital.

"Is this a temptation or a dream come true?" I wondered.

I had daydreams about becoming a Christian missionary someday. Because I enjoyed myself with the secular medical mission my brother Jun organized, I realized the possibility. We had been successful in the area of family planning. But there was much more to do as a Christian doctor.

Public health issues for the Philippines included family planning. Before I joined our family medical mission, I trained with Planned Parenthood for one month after graduation. In the Philippines it is different—the country does not allow abortions. The scope of care for Planned Parenthood there was teaching about family planning.

My Chinese suitor struck a positive chord embedded in my mind. I wanted to become a medical missionary. When I was a fourth-year medical student, I went to an Overseas Missionary Fellowship (of Baptist background). The two American missionaries reached out to the students. They had a place for us to go. I enjoyed my spare time in Christian fellowship. Mrs. Baskett always was there. She was my friend. We would do puzzles, play games, solve crossword puzzles and meet other students.

Other Christians went there, too. Many of them were

international students from other countries. They often had nothing to do, and this place was welcoming. My Chinese suitor came to this center. We met. He became attracted to me. I found it odd that he was reading *Of Human Bondage* by William Somerset Maugham, a medical doctor.

He was Chinese. His family moved from China during the Green Revolution. They fled to Thailand. His father, a businessman, thrived in Thailand. They had since expanded their business to Taiwan. Their canning factory exported to maybe 30 countries. Also they made meat and seafood jerky. He showed me pictures of the factory, trying to convince me to allow courtship. The factory had 500 employees.

I tell you, it was something to think about seriously. I thought he might be the husband God selected for me. I wanted only God's best. He even met my father to seek his approval to court me. I was finishing medical school soon, which my father said was my priority.

His father wanted him to earn a master's degree in economics in the USA. After the Philippine experience to improve his English, he had more years of study in America. So many people from Asia came to the Philippines to study and to practice their English because we are English speaking, and then they became professionals in the United States.

What was I to make of his "golden cage" offer? He was attracted to me like an obsession. He was always coming to the center. I could not escape his attention. His courting was not welcome. While I didn't have a boyfriend and was already 25 years old, I just was not in love with him. For one thing, he was not Christian.

Pleading with me, he said he would become a Christian, would go to church. But I did not believe his protestations. Logically my father taught that men will say one thing to win a wife but later renege on their promises. Besides, I understood, the Chinese have this idea that they keep their women in the home. Definitely not me!!

I was and am not that kind of person. I was more American in my attitude, even more than Filipino. While conservative in Christian belief, I could not be kept at home. I wanted to practice medicine. My father always told us, "Study hard and work so the men will not just treat you badly." My father always drilled us too, the oldest to the youngest sitting on a long bench, as my father was a judge. He asked us individually, "Are you going to study or have boyfriends?" Of course we wanted to study, you know. So we promised. That's why I didn't have a boyfriend, I was scared. Not only that, but I was also choosy.

My internalized ideal guy did not match with my Chinese suitor. First, the one I could love must already love the Lord. He must be more mature in his faith walk than I. So nothing really happened. Maybe I was just his magnificent obsession. And he awakened my wishful thinking.

Imagine this, for five years he pursued me. He got mad at himself because he didn't understand why he was attracted to me. I resisted him, I said "no" again and again.

My thoughts at the time were: "I'm not getting married, I have other ideas, I have other plans. I am going to the United States of America. My vision is to come to this land of opportunity where missionaries come from. I idealize America as a Christian country. Freedom is there. I can do what I want to do, nobody will tell me what to do. I can be what I want to be. I can work hard. I will work hard and be what I can be. That's my lifestyle, that's what I want my life to be."

Summum bonum! I desired God's best! No golden cage for me.

POBRENG MALIPAYON
"The Happy Poor"

My understanding of God grew as my medical education progressed. I realized that when I accepted Jesus in my heart as a teenager, God directed my life. Just like a soldier joins military service and begins with boot camp, so did I.

After formal medical education at Far Eastern University, I served a year as an intern at the Filipino Veterans Hospital. Many times I helped care for Filipino soldiers who were fighting with the Muslims in the southern island of Mindanao. Our surgical service operated on them. It was sobering to see the wounds of war but was great clinical experience. Surprising to some is the fact that our veterans hospital had an active obstetrics service where we were required to deliver 40 babies by year's end and before we could graduate from medical school. We had babies born every day.

Then I graduated in 1967 as a medical doctor, passing the Filipino Medical National Board Exam. I felt the power of God and rejoiced. My parents deserve honor for helping me each step of my life.

When I graduated, my brother Nemesio Ganan, Jr., (known affectionately as Jun), who was a politician at that time running for the provincial board, was very ambitious. He formed a medical mission. I was a new doctor, his wife Guady was a doctor, and my sister Bella was a nurse. He recruited all of us, and we called it *Pobreng Malipayon*, which means "The Happy Poor."

My brother rented a motorized boat and we went from island to island. I enjoyed myself. I had daydreams about becoming a missionary someday. My sisters all agreed that we should. In fact, my younger sister wanted to become a doctor. But that's what we dreamed about, that we would become missionaries.

The medical mission, while not religious but secular,

did help the poor. Practicing the healing arts let me see that God heals. While I think my brother's intention was to make himself more popular as a politician, and it accomplished that, we served the Bible prescription to love our neighbor. If a Filipino hears *"Pobreng Malipayon"* in the Visayan region, he identifies the slogan with my brother.

The story of my delivery of twins as the ship doctor occurred at the end of our medical mission, serving from island to island. See the story "Ferry Ship Doctor" in Greenbrier's book *Stories of a West Virginia Doctor for Kith and Kin*.

Jun eventually became a member of the Philippine Parliament. His wife eventually became one of the Philippine presidential house staff doctors. During our time at the medical mission, my younger sister Bella was our staff nurse and I served as a staff doctor. We both eventually immigrated to America. Stay tuned for more of that adventure. Our Ganan family continued to serve our people. My older sister Priscilla, a family nutritionist, could not join us because of her job in public health as a nutritionist. She has had her God's Boot Camp experience adopting starving children.

We had a great time serving with *Pobreng Malipayon*. Dreams of becoming medical missionaries together inspired us all. One of my sisters even went to medical school but did not like it and stopped at the third year. Encouraged to be in medical field, she then went to dental school and was doing well, but disliked it also and stopped altogether. She had her own dreams, following the calling in her own way.

Missions became engraved in my heart. Later on when I was in the USA, opportunity presented itself. I volunteered with *Amigos Internationales,* going on mission to Belize. God's plan for me has led from one adventurous story to another.

COMING TO AMERICA

EAST VERSUS WEST

I came to the United States at the end of October 1970. Before that time, I had a classmate that was maybe a little interested in me. The way it was in the Philippines during my time, the man serenaded the woman he liked. He would come to your house with another friend or two and would sing love songs to you. Then he would tell the maid or servants the girl he was interested in, because there were often many women in the house. I knew it was Ben. He was interested in me, but I wasn't particularly interested in him. Yes, he was a Christian, thus fitting my standard as a Christian guy. But he was adopted. It should not matter, but I was too proud at that time. Plus, I had my own ideas about what I wanted to do. So anyway, he serenaded me and sometimes came to visit me.

At that time we didn't date. Our childhood was extended. We had beach parties and were still climbing trees in high school. I was just a girl at 15 years old! I was actually even delayed in my growing up. Pubescence was late. I never missed a gym class due to a menstrual period.

But being serenaded like that at night—what great fun! We were very formal. After singing, the boy and girl could sit in the living room and chat innocently. They sat on opposite sides of a center table, and there was a chaperone.

How sheltered we were in the Philippines. I never even stayed in a hotel. It was the bad girls that went to hotels. So people there were very hospitable and they would keep you in their homes. No one stayed in a hotel, not like here.

Weddings are grand celebrations in the Philippine Islands. When my brother Jun got married, I was a bridesmaid and Ben, who had serenaded me, was my partner. My mother and father had José B. Laurel, Jr., the Speaker of the House of the Philippines, attend the wedding. Laurel caused commotion in our town of Odiongan when he flew in by helicopter. And Philippine

Vice-President Fernando Lopez was a godfather at the wedding of my brother. In fact, a week after the wedding, I accompanied my brother and his wife to dinner with Lopez.

Even with deep cultural roots in the Philippines, I determined to go on my own, leaving the East for the West. I desired to make life decisions on my own. America as an ideal was what called me to great adventure. But what trouble did I get into!!! My, what a life! I can look back and wonder.

"God's Boot Camp" is what I call my amazing life. If God did not take care of me, I would have been lost forever! However, I can testify that God truly is faithful and true! He is all I had and He will always be my Lord!

COMING TO AMERICA

Mother had left her remote northern Luzon mountain village of La Union to come to Manila to study in a university at a time young women just did not do that. Now Mother and Father were granting my desire to come to America, the land of opportunity. Very few young women from Asia had the chance I had. I wanted to work hard, to set big goals and to accomplish much.

I told my parents that I wanted to come to America, and they agreed to let me go. Before that, my older sister wanted to come to America on her own, too, but they didn't let her. But when it came to me, they let me. I don't know why, but they did. Maybe it was because I was a doctor by that time. Doctors were welcomed to come to America with open arms.

I had dreamed of America all along, for I had known American missionaries. They were visionaries. They were my ideal. What a country! What a people! America was a Christian nation in my eyes. I read a lot about how great Americans are. They are very helpful, they are very kind. I said I wanted to be part of that culture. They say America is the greatest country in the world—I wanted to be there. So it was my dream. I was excited

"Ready or not, here I come! America look out!" I wrote excitedly to my pen-pal. We had began writing each other in the third grade through a concerted effort by Philippine and American churches to unite our two nations via a pen-pal partnership. My American friend was Roanne Warren. We wrote each other for several years then lost touch. As I prepared for my American adventure, I wrote her a letter. I didn't receive any answer back. I thought she had probably married and moved away.

Thinking ahead, I decided I would come as an immigrant to the USA with a permanent visa, not a student visa. Partly it was a bureaucratic thing, because with a student visa I would have to renew it every year. But as a young professional, I felt my goal of Christian medical missions would be best served by having a permanent visa. My citizenship would remain Filipino, but I could go in and out of the United States as I liked with a green card. So I believed it best to wait for my permanent visa. God opened the door for me. I only waited one year. Our two countries were very close in the 1960s. My year of waiting had been well spent working for my brother's medical mission *Pobreng Malipayon* as part of the staff. I also worked as a doctor at the Vasquez Clinic, a private industrial medical clinic that provided urgent care and gave physical exams to foreigners, especially those arriving in ships that came to the Philippines via Manila Bay. We also provided physicals for those applying to immigrate to the United States.

The night before leaving, I was apprehensive about coming to America. I was really restless and excited both. I wanted to come to America. I said, "Wow, I will be free to do what I want to do!" Nobody would tell me what to do. In our culture we were very much protected. While I liked it, and I still like it even now, freedom is a powerful draw. I believed I could handle it.

However, at the same time I was scared, because I would not have my family with me. But I was depending on my profession. My medical studies had bolstered my confidence. So, 28 years old, fancy free, and bold as a peacock: "Uncle Sam, here I come!"

Many blessings were counted. How amazing! Certainly I did not want anything to stop me from coming to America. The devil has tricks he can play, but God is sovereign. The night before my departure, everybody in our house was asleep, including my parents in the next room. I was in my bed. Somebody was making a noise at my window. I didn't know what it was, so I opened the window. What I saw scared me. There was a stepladder leaning against the wall. So I screamed to my parents, and they woke up. Everybody woke up, and we went downstairs to look at the ladder. We didn't see anybody, just the ladder.

Up to now, I don't know who it was or what the purpose was. My suspicious mind says that perhaps a suitor was trying to break into the room where I usually slept. Perhaps he inquired from the servants the location of my room. In our culture, I could have been a victim of a shotgun wedding. A man found in a woman's room was a real honor-breaking situation. My, not me!

Well, that was an event in my life that could have stopped me getting to the USA. Really, God protected me even as He placed major challenges in front of me. I was in God's Boot Camp. Each day that I survived, I was growing as a person.

CRASH LANDING

Tablas Island connects to the outside world by ferry boat and by airplane. My parents honored their doctor daughter by letting me take the airplane. This was a recent service just added to the island, as previously the only mode of transportation to and from the island was the ferry. From Manila I would connect to the international flight to the United States. My parents took the boat because they had so many of my things to carry, which I could not take with me on the local flight. Baggage limits on the small airplane were impractical. We would say our final bon voyage at the airport in Manila.

The ferry was less expensive, yet taking the boat was very cumbersome. All the oinking pigs, the clucking chickens, mixed with the people! And the folding Army cots left over from World War II were all the passengers had for rest. There were no cabins. Everything was spread out. Then if one vomited, everybody vomited. I remember that very well.

"What a blessing to fly," I thought. The airplane was full. I was in the aisle seat on the right-hand side of the airplane. Another young woman sat beside me. We had about 100 people on board our propeller-type airplane.

My mother's best friend, who was a Christian lady of the Baptist denomination, sat maybe four seats ahead on the left side, the other aisle of the airplane. We flew from our airport on the east side of Tablas Island. I kept looking out the airplane window, seeing my island for perhaps the last time. I contemplated about going to America; I was really so excited. And how exciting it was to fly in the airplane!

But as we arrived at the Manila airport, our plane kept circling around and around. I wondered why we did not approach the airport and land. The pilot was just roaming around. Then the captain announced, "We are going to crash land. The landing gear of the airplane won't come out. So we have to nose dive. We have to use up all the gas now so that when we crash land we will not explode."

So everybody was crying, "It's the end, we will crash land, what will we do?" Because it's a Catholic country, everybody was praying, "Hail Mary full of grace," and everybody was crying for their families.

I couldn't cry. I just said, "Thank You God for Your peace in my heart. Thank You that I am redeemed. Thank You that I am Christian."

I was thinking and praying more for my family. I prayed that my parents would be okay without me, since I would never see them again.

"God, I'm too young to die now. I won't see America! I hope it doesn't hurt so much when I die. I hope it doesn't hurt or burn. I just want to die and wake up in Your Presence.

"Thank You, God, for my life up to this point. Thank You for the world that You made for me." Then I looked out the window and absorbed as much as I could of the nice world that God made and thanked God for it. The stewardess came around and gave us small pillows to have to curl up into.

Next, the Captain said to take all the sharps from our pockets and take off our eyeglasses, so I took my glasses off. I didn't have pockets for sharps, it was just my glasses. And I curled myself up against the pillow on my knee and waited for the worst.

Then the airplane was landing, so I was closed my eyes right before impact. The landing was bumpy, but we didn't explode; we were still alive. I opened up my eyes and the captain announced, "We are safe!"

He landed the airplane in the rice farm beside the airport, and we didn't explode. We were met by police cars and an ambulance, and we were allowed to get out. All the passengers got out of there. We were alive!

Looking back, I remember the day before my departure.

I had asked my father to ask our local pastor, Pastor Danganan, to come pray with me, asking God to bless me on my journey to America. Our pastor came, and his prayer helped influence my life, giving me the courage to go on to the unknown. He quoted Jesus' words in Matthew 28:20: "Lo, I am with you always, even unto the end of the world."

And God was with me. I shall not forget the crash landing lesson from God's Boot Camp: "Trust God."

BECOMING BRAVE

I was so naïve, so starry-eyed, so awed about my new environment, America!

I had great expectations. My faith in this new, free country was boundless. I came for growth opportunities.

Yes, I knew from the Bible that there can be attacks of the devil at times like this. But my faith in God was firm. For I believed I could be what I wanted to be with hard work and guidance from God, even if my family was not around.

Several events curbed my confidence. One happening was the ladder incident. I never knew who put that ladder from the yard to my upstairs bedroom the night before my departure for America. Apparently I scared off the perpetrator. If he had succeeded in entering my bedroom, I might have been forced into an unwanted marriage.

Being a cosmopolitan young lady always ready to shop almost caused me to miss my departure flight. The day before my flight for the USA, I went for last-minute shopping in Escolta, then the trendy place to shop. I drove my brother's Renault car. (I had obtained an international driver's license.)

About 6:00 p.m. the rain poured. Traffic snarled as badly as Manila city traffic does. Suddenly, a taxi rear-ended me, and the Renault got a dimple in the bumper. My, my. I never told my brother about the problem, as it would have delayed my leaving. I rationalized that the dimple was noticeable only if closer inspection was done. "Don't ask, don't tell" was the strategy I employed.

Most seriously, one month before my flight to the USA, I was a witness to an error by a student nurse that might have aggravated my nephew's cerebral damage. He was being treated with powerful antibiotics for possible encephalitis. I was sitting by his bedside, asleep. He was groaning and I woke up. I then saw that the student nurse had used an old, partially-used IV bottle which looked muddy. It was most likely contaminated, and her action was certainly against safety protocol. I had been asleep at the time and only realized what she had done after the fact.

We discussed the potential harm and our legal remedy. In the end my parents decided not to sue the hospital. Surely the student nurse's future would have been destroyed. The tragedy was that his young brain was already severely damaged.

With regard to my future, it would have delayed or stopped my coming to America, in order for me to testify in court. Certainly all this weighed on my mind as I made final preparation for coming to America at the end of October 1970 with my classmate and friend Dulce Amor Pagarigan.

Bravely I flew with Dulce on schedule. We stopped over in Honolulu for a day at her relatives' place. She and I then flew into Los Angeles, California, staying with my town mate, Evelyn Tradejas, from Tablas Island. After a week, Dulce flew to New York to find her own new life.

God gave boldness to this little South Pacific native filled with wonder and awe at actually being in America. My faith in God sustained me as I prayed for Him to prepare a way where there was no way. Let me say again, I prayed a lot! I was scared but really very optimistic and confident. Young and hopeful . . .

LIFE, LIBERTY,
AND THE PURSUIT OF HAPPINESS

After I flew to California from the Philippines, I set about discovering this land of my dreams. Knowing God is everywhere, even California, I sought out the Angelus Temple. This is the mother church of the Foursquare Gospel Church. I wanted to start my new life with prayer. They had a "Prayer Tower" which I telephoned.

Though I was alone in America, I was very confident. My faith in God sustained me. Not happy to only call them, I set out to visit the church to worship and to ask for prayer in person. I don't know how God managed it, but I found the right buses. However, the church had no mid-week worship. It was open anyway, so I went inside. Nobody was there. I saw the prayer room and went inside. I put my three requests on a piece of paper. One: to have a job, a training job for doctors, not just any job. Two: to make a decision about marrying my Chinese suitor I had met in the Philippines. Three: to pass my test for the ECFMG (Educational Council for Foreign Medical Graduates) so I could apply to a training hospital in the USA.

Everything worked out, considering this was my first time separated from my father and family. Even living arrangements appeared "arranged" by divine plan. I stayed with another girl, Evelyn Fradejas, from Tablas Island, Philippines. Her younger sister Lilia was my younger sister Edna's grade school classmate and good friend. (In fact, Evelyn and I saw each other again two years ago in the Philippines. She was vacationing there, and I told her how grateful I am for God putting me in her arms, in her apartment at that time.)

Really without being asked, Evelyn volunteered, "Oh, if you want a good job, there is a job to be a billing clerk for Blue Cross Blue Shield. It's medical, you can do that, but don't tell them you're a doctor. They won't accept you.

You'll be over-qualified." So I lied. I felt really guilty about that, because my father was very strict about that. We were not supposed to lie. And I lied because I wanted a job and I listened to Satan's direction instead of trusting God. I didn't tell them about being a doctor. Then after two weeks of training, I stopped. I didn't even call them, I just stopped going, because I felt guilty. And I felt even worse because our supervisor was very nice to us, a very nice lady.

Then I talked to the Prayer Tower staff about my suitor dilemma. They said, "What are you praying for?"

I said, "Someone wants to marry me and I'm not sure if I should marry him. The guy said, 'Five years you have known me, you should know, you already know me.' He is a very honorable guy."

I called two nights in a row, because my suitor had said, "You have three days to make your decision. After that I am gone. When I am gone, I am gone. You cry, you cry alone. Remember now you don't have your family here, I am the only one you know." So I got scared, too. He had millions plus all that kind of support that I needed.

As I will tell in the story "God's Choice," all worked out.

Finally, my third prayer was answered positively with my medical test success. That opened the door for my internship at Pittsburgh's Saint Margaret's Hospital. As I flew out of California, I knew God's Boot Camp training was making me a stronger Christian. I felt full of Life, felt the Liberty that comes with Christ, and felt ready to pursue more Happiness.

GOD'S CHOICE

My persistent Chinese suitor had given me three days to decide if I would marry him. He pressed for an answer to his pleas for marriage. He had waited five years and would continue to wait another five years, but only if he knew I agreed to marry him when I was ready.

My mother and father had taught me to seek God's wisdom in major life decisions. My father held family council meetings when we could gather. After coming to America, I faced many choices alone but still used God's Word.

In God's Army we need reinforcements to win a tough battle. So as I wrestled with my decision, in addition to seeking prayer from the Angelus Temple's Prayer Tower, I called the missionaries I had come to know in the Philippines. The Basketts, who were the Baptists Overseas missionaries, knew my suitor.

I called them there in Oregon long distance and said, "Mom, pray for me."

Mrs. Baskett said, "What about? Where are you?"

I said, "I'm in L.A."

"Oh, you're in L.A."

I said, "Mom," and I named the guy, "is still pursuing me."

"Until now?" She couldn't believe it. "Araceli, until now?" She couldn't believe it.

"Yes, ma'am. I don't know what to do. Please pray for me."

"Yes, I will pray for you."

And that's it. These missionaries prayed for me as I challenged God Himself.

I had studied the Bible and understood that my life partner must be a Christian. But I wavered in the face of my suitor's demand for an answer. So anyway, I had the Bible, a King James Version I brought from the Philippines with me. I said, "God, I believed You all my life. I don't have my father here, but You are my Father. My father is not here. I'm not Mary, I'm not holy enough for You to appear to me or for an angel to tell me what to do, but here are Your words," I said. I showed Him my Bible. I said, "Here are Your words. Tell me what to do. You can tell me by Your words, through this; You don't have to appear to me, because I'm not holy."

You know what? I closed my eyes—they say you aren't supposed to do that but I did it anyway, at that time I was desperate—and put my finger somewhere and looked. You know where it led? II Corinthians 6:14: "Be ye not unequally yoked together with unbelievers: for what fellowship hath righteousness with unrighteousness?"

I tell you, I was scared! I was actually scared. You know, because I knew that verse. They preached that in the church, they did. "Be ye not unequally yoked with unbelievers . . . " but I couldn't believe it, I really couldn't believe that's the verse God would give me.

So I said, "God, is it really You talking to me?" I wouldn't believe it, because it could have been circumstance only.

I said, "God, You have to give me another verse to support what You said to me." I closed the Bible, closed my eyes again, opened it somewhere and pointed. And when I looked, I just cried, cried, cried. I lost my energy. I fell on the carpet and said, "Yes Father, I will obey You and wait for the man You have for me." You know what the verse was? It was exactly the same verse! How can that be? How can it be? It was not circumstance to me anymore. It couldn't be. It was God talking to me.

Because I challenged Him, "If this is You talking to me, give me a verse."

And He said, "I said what I said!" So I cried, cried, cried. I was determined I was not going to marry this obsessive suitor.

41

I now knew my answer was no. When my suitor returned on the third day, I said to him, "Thank you for loving me, but I cannot marry you."

He was very sad and he left. My girlfriend's apartment had a veranda, a porch. I was standing there watching him drive away with tears in my eyes. I was full of compassion for my suitor and uncertainty of my own future.

Through God's Word and through prayer I gave my final answer: "No!" Another lesson learned in God's Boot Camp made me a stronger woman. But after that, you know what, I went through more hardships.

MY TEARS JUST FLOWED

My tears just flowed! Because now I was alone; I had nobody else. What would I do in the United States? Yet I was all for adventure on my own.

The chapter of my life was closed. Finally I had said to my Chinese suitor, "No, I cannot marry you." I was flattered. I didn't really want to completely say no, because I wanted to give myself a chance. I may have been making a mistake. I would never have millions. I didn't even know what that was. I thought, "Anything I don't have, I won't miss." I said to myself, "I will work hard as a doctor. I won't be poor, you know. If I work hard, I won't be poor, I will have something to eat." So I was comfortable with that.

My Chinese suitor gave the deadline. So when he came on the third day for the verdict, I told him, "No, I can't marry you."

After that, I felt happy. Continually I praised God. "Father, I will obey You and wait for the man You have for me." That's what I said. I was 28 years old and had never had a boyfriend. You're wondering, whats was wrong with me? A girl that age should be married already and have a family already, and here I was roaming around. On the other hand, I felt like I had a new life now.

Miraculously, I passed my medical education test. I didn't study but I passed my test. God answered my prayer. I got an acceptance to Pittsburgh's St. Margaret's Hospital for my internship. They sent me an airplane ticket to come for free. So now I was happy because I had a plane ticket to go. They said they would meet me at the airport.

Bittersweet is the final page of my story on this chapter of my life. My now-former suitor called. "Can I take you to the airport?"

I said, "No, I'll take a taxi, that's fine."

"No, please," he begged, "let me take you to the

43

airport."

Then I thought to myself: "This man is honorable, he deserves to be treated well." But I was still determined about my own life, that he was not the one. But you know, I let him hold my hand all the way from the apartment to the airport. I normally wouldn't let him hold my hand, but I thought, "He's a nice guy, you know, holding his hand probably won't kill me, so okay, hold my hand." I just kept quiet all the way to the airport. In the old days, the people saying goodbye could go to the gate. So he was sitting there beside me. We were not talking; we were just deep in thought together. I was very peaceful. I didn't know what he was thinking.

Then he said, "May I kiss you?" But I felt like everyone was looking at me. I wasn't used to that.

So I told him, "Here," and I pointed to my cheek. He kissed me on the cheek. Then I went to the accordion to go to the airplane. I looked back and he was standing there looking at me, and that's the last time I saw him in my life.

And as I was there on the airplane, sitting there, I don't know what I was thinking, but suddenly when the airplane flew, I felt like two big weights on my shoulders fell off. I felt very, very light. I was very happy. I don't know, I was just happy for no reason. That load fell off and I was very light. I was just happy, period. I was now free.

When I landed at the airport in the early evening, nobody was there to meet me. I waited and waited and nobody was with me, so I had to take a taxi to St. Margaret's Hospital. I was scared to death because I'd never been alone in a taxi like that.

Anyway, I was so happy to open a new chapter of my life. Fellow interns and staff probably wondered, "Oh look at Dr. Ganan, she's so happy!" Indeed, I was just happy! Because now I was free. I didn't have anybody to worry about. I was just beaming with joy.

TIMES OF HARDSHIP
IN PENNSYLVANIA

MUSIC HEALS

The *Pittsburgh Press* newspaper featured me in an article as the "Singing Doctor," due to my weekly musical programs for patients in St. Margaret's Hospital.

God had miraculously provided a guitar for me in California. I attended a party with some Americans. One man introduced himself as Gibson, but I did not catch his first name. He said he had a guitar.

I said, "Oh, you have a guitar?"

He said, "Yes, I own Gibson Guitars." He was the owner. But I didn't know anything about Gibson Guitars at that time.

I said, "Yeah, I play guitar a little bit. I'm not too good."

"Oh, you play guitar?" Gibson smiled.

"Yeah."

"Well, if I sell you my guitar, would you get it?"

"How much would it cost?"

"$45."

"Yeah!"

Gibson said, "I planned to give it to my girlfriend," (he had a Japanese girlfriend) "but if you want it, I'll sell it to you for $45." And he even gave me a free hard case for it.

You know what, I was so happy to have a guitar. I prayed, "God, use it for Your glory. I can sing a little bit. I'm not a very good singer, but I can sing a little bit. Use it for Your glory."

And you know, it occurred to me, when I was in Pittsburgh, to give a program for the patients. I used the guitar, and I sang for the patients once a week. A doctor who was there doing his family practice residency, Dr. Charles Kuhn, played the piano with me. He was a very good piano player and a professing Christian. His piano playing was answered prayer.

Charlie's life story was tragic. He married, and the next

day during their honeymoon they had a car accident. His wife died instantly. He was in the ICU for one month. As a result of the accident, his left eye was sunken, he had a disfigured face, and he took so many medicines, multiple medicines, and when he walked he had to put his hands on the wall to keep his balance. Maybe he had seizures.

Still on my mind was my desire for a Christian husband. I told God, "I told You I would wait for the man You have for me. Is he the one? Because he's a Christian, he plays the piano for me. But there's a problem—he is not the one I myself would choose. But if he is the one for me, I'll take him. If he is the one You are giving me, I'll take him."

Certainly I really, really yielded to God, but I knew there would be resistance from my family. How to explain this to my parents? But I was determined. I thought: "I am in America now, I can plan my own life. I am free. I can explain to my parents later on. I'm in America, they're too far away to do anything."

I prayed, but then nothing happened except for the wonderful musical programs for our patients. Together our music healed.

MICKEY MOUSE AND MORE

One of the most visited places in America is Disney World in Orlando, Florida. As a new green-card-holding American, during my one-week vacation as a medical rotating intern at St. Margaret's Hospital, I wanted to see Disney World. It had just opened in 1971. The place was a work-in-progress. But I wanted to go. Everybody wanted to go to Orlando, to Disney World. "Mickey Mouse and friends: Here I come, ready or not!"

So I took a bus, having been given help with arrangements by the international student organization minster, Mr. Fred Wolfe. He helped me find places to stay with three families along the bus route to Orlando. A special salute to the Americans who were so kind and hospitable to this young recruit to God's Boot Camp.

After that short vacation all alone, I prayed for a companion for future vacations. How very lonely I was. Having to ask somebody to take my picture with my new $40 camera was the pits. Overall, though, I had a blast.

The Greyhound bus route included a stop in Louisville, Kentucky, where I stayed overnight with Nettie White, a dear old Christian lady. Next I stayed with the Crowfoots in Atlanta for one night. The Crowfoots are Christian saints, from my perspective. More about them later.

Now this is really God's timing. The Stonestreet Family from West Virginia was in Atlanta at the time that I stayed with the Crowfoots. They had brought their daughter to a Christian psychologist for consultation in Atlanta. Later they "adopted" me when I came to Charleston, West Virginia, for my pediatric residency. Finally, I stayed with a Christian family in Florida while touring Disney World alone. Yes, I met Mickey Mouse!

I loved my experience. Looking back, I see God's protective hand guiding me on my trip. America is the land of the free and home of the brave—including me!

"GOD SAYS YOU WILL GO FAR"

During one of my weekly musical programs for the patients at St. Margaret's Hospital, I witnessed, giving my testimony. Afterward, an African-American man approached me and in a prophetic utterance declared with joy, "Dr. Ganan, God says you will go far." How that message has comforted me.

It also has given me a chance to laugh. Now when anything goes wrong with my life, I say to myself, "Sure, I really got far!" Actually, I have gone far for a South Pacific Island girl.

With my belief in healing from the Foursquare Gospel background, which included founder Aimee Semple McPherson (also known as Sister Aimee, 1890-1944), I was excited to know that Pittsburgh was the headquarters for a famous faith healer. At that time, Kathryn Kuhlman created quite a stir in Pittsburgh.

My fellow physician and the pianist for my musical program, Dr. Charles Kuhn, said, "People who believe in that are crazy."

But I believed in it. I just kept quiet. I just didn't say anything. Dr. Kuhn didn't realize he was the object of my prayers. I would accept him if God gave him to me, not just as a pianist but also a help meet.

One day we were eating, and he said he was going to stop playing for me. He said, "Nothing in this country is free." I thought he was talking about the free food in the cafeteria. Then he said, "Heil Hitler."

I had heard about Hitler. I also raised my hand like he did because Dr. Kuhn greeted me like that. I thought it was a joke, you know. It was such a bad joke, though; I didn't even realize how bad Hitler was.

Time passed quickly that year at St. Margaret's Hospital. Working with the house staff was basically a good experience. But we had a few improvements we thought needed to be made for future doctors in training. I was actually assigned the job of spokesperson for all the interns. Probably I was too bold. I was new in America and I didn't know what a spokesperson did. To me it was an honor, and I was happy to speak up like my father had taught us to do in the Philippines.

One issue with medicolegal ramifications involved assigning interns in the emergency room without supervision. We were just there to work. Most of us were doctors already, we knew what to do, but the medicines here were different, and many of the interns were not American born. We were mainly foreign medical graduates. All the interns signed a petition requesting supervision,and I gave it to the director. The secretary of the director kept asking me who initiated it. Well, I wasn't going to tell anybody about who did it, because it was right, what we were doing.

I got far—right!

MARTIAL LAW PROCLAIMED

Proclamation № 1081 was the declaration of martial law in the Philippines by President Ferdinand E. Marcos. It became effective throughout the entire country on September 21, 1972, and was announced to the public two days later. After that date I got a letter from the Philippines from my older sister mailed to my new address in Philadelphia, Pennsylvania. My new residency in psychiatry at Thomas Jefferson University Hospital was just underway. (I began on July 1, 1972.)

Nothing was mentioned about homeland problems in Sister Precy's letter. The stamp on the envelope mailed from the Philippines was a poison stamp—the skull and bones with a black background, like on a poison. I learned in the news that martial law was proclaimed in the Philippines. So I was concerned because my family was there, but I trusted God and was not too scared.

Naturally curious, I talked to every Filipino I knew to see if they had received a letter with that kind of stamp. They said no. Nobody else had such a warning. So I was just baffled. But there were no more letters at that time. It took one month for the letters to arrive.

My life had been hectic as I wrapped up my year at St. Margaret's Hospital. After being the spokesperson for the interns, the secretary advised me, "Dr. Ganan, don't ask for a letter of recommendation." My medical education director was upset with me. But I stuck to my decision not to implicate the other interns when the director asked me to reveal to him who had started the petition demanding proper supervision. I carried the spokesperson role as a badge of honor.

Another time I ended up in a culturally awkward situation. Women physicians are taught to be alert to sexual innuendo. We must use our women's intuition. Even if I imagine too much, I must still stand on my gut feeling.

Anyway, I was in the library one day. Nobody was there and then our director came in. He was reading something.

Throughout the year I had thought of him as a nice guy, a decent Catholic man. He said, "My dear, come here." I heard that word "dear." A red flag immediately raised up in my mind. I didn't go.

Ever since that I avoided him. Then I was told not to seek his recommendation. Certainly I was on shaky ground. I didn't know where to go. It was very hard for a foreign doctor to find a residency program. I applied to internal medicine, as pediatrics (my eventual specialty) wasn't really my first choice at that time. But I didn't receive any acceptance.

Faced with the prospect of going home, I jumped at a residency opening up in Thomas Jefferson University Hospital in Philadelphia. This was for psychiatry. So I applied for it. They took me without requiring recommendations.

My thinking about pursuing the psychiatry residency was this: Other doctors sometimes have two or three specialties. Therefore, I could always go back to what my interest was. At least I wouldn't have lost anything; it was still another field.

My relationship with God deepened through all these tribulations. God had me in boot camp for sure.

ALABASTER CITY WITH TEARS

O beautiful for patriot dream
That sees beyond the years
Thine alabaster cities gleam
Undimmed by human tears!
America! America!

"America the Beautiful"
Katharine Lee Bates

Oh how I love America! Oh how I've shed tears here!

Philadelphia is such a big city. Even though Manila has more people, there I felt the closeness of family and friends. The City of Brotherly Love may have gleamed brighter, but it proved frightening. I was there for my psychiatry residency. For starters, I was assigned to the 11th floor of a dorm. One day one of the residents where I lived said that her mother was coming and she didn't have a bed for her. She knew I had two beds in my room and asked if I could accommodate her. Sure, you know, you want to help somebody, why not, especially another resident. She was from Central America.

So I put her up in my place, in my other bed. She was a strange woman. At night, she would sit up and would mumble around and say, "Someone even jumped out of the window." Those words reverberated in my brain.

I said, "'Someone even jumped out of the window?' It's the 11th floor—they would be dead." Anyway, she was very strange. I brushed off the incident. I had much to be dealing with beside the comments from an elderly woman. After three days she left. I was relieved that she had to leave.

In September, my residency rotation changed to a rotation in the emergency room. And nobody was supervising me there, either. I tell you, that place was crazy. It's a city and they had people there who were crazy, maybe on drugs, and there was no one supervising me. I didn't know what to do. So you know what I did as a Christian? I prayed for them. Some of them got well, really.

Maybe the nurse told my supervisor about my plight of being unsupervised. Anyway, I also complained to my supervisor. I didn't have an attending to help me. I was scared myself.

As I write this memoir, I can feel the tension building just recalling my situation. Martial law being declared in the Philippines gave me grave pause. My analysis of the situation was that I felt it was safer to stay put in the USA since I did not know what martial law was or what it was doing to the country. I thought of tanks rolling around the streets and people being imprisoned or killed; I was really not too sure. I kept praying to God, feeling His comfort in my heart, and life went on. The letter with the poison stamp disappeared, but I am sure I did not throw it away. Gone! Where did it go? Well, God knows.

I went to my director the day after I had a rough day in the emergency room. There was a big rectangular desk. I was on the other side. I was going to tell him I needed supervision there, complain about my whole ordeal.

Then he said, "Come here, I want to show you something." I went around the table to see what it was. He was pointing to his knees. He was sitting, opening and closing his knees, and he was pointing down there. I got scared. I didn't know why he was doing this. I tell you, I got out of there quickly. I don't know what he meant by it. It seemed sexual, but I wasn't sure. I didn't know what he meant.

The next day, my life was about to turn upside-down. I was eating at the cafeteria. I thought about what happened, and I thought then that I was in danger. Usually I am brave and not easily scared.

I was just eating lunch there, and suddenly I trembled. I was shaking. My mind got out of line. My mind said I was going to be shot, or that maybe something happened to my family in the Philippines. I was really thinking something was happening in the Philippines or somebody was going to shoot me. I closed my eyes because I was afraid somebody was shooting me. It was crazy, got crazy. My mind went wrong and I was shaking. I thought, "Oh no, what's wrong with me?" I stood up to try to call my family. I wanted to find a phone so I could call them. But I didn't know where a phone was. I could not locate a phone, and I knew there was no phone anyway on my home island in 1972. So I stood up. I didn't finish my food and just got out to go to my room to lie down, just to relax maybe.

I was in a panic state. Somebody followed me, a female. She saw my situation and stopped me from going back to my apartment and recommended that I go to the emergency room, which I did.

I was yelling. I don't know why. I was really out of my mind. Then I went to the emergency room, and they didn't even ask me why I was upset. My director was there and he ordered a shot for me, I don't know, I guess to make me very sleepy. He ordered that I should be given something to calm me down, a shot. I was very sleepy after that.

Also present was a psychologist named Barney. He provided emotional support. We had the beginnings of a friendship. I was very comfortable with him. In my panic state I pleaded, "Barney, please don't go."

So he said, "I'm staying." The doctors said I had to go somewhere for hospitalization. They would arrange ambulance transport. I needed to rest. But I would not be allowed to stay at Thomas Jefferson Hospital because I was a resident there. My mind interpreted the emergency physician's decision as sending me into danger.

From my University days in Manila I had been very careful because Mrs. Baskett, the Christian missionary, told me all the time, "Keep yourself pure."

I believed she taught rightly. She said, "You will never regret that."

I said, "Yes, ma'am."

But I was in the ER afraid they were going to take me somewhere really bad. So I clung to Barney, "Please don't go." The doctor said he was going to send me in an ambulance to a nice place, instead of being placed upstairs.

I was a doctor. Why did they not let me talk about my fears? Why was there no medical history taken? What was happening? How about a drug screen in case I had been poisoned? I was just being dumped! Even my director ordered an injection without a history of medication allergy. Soon I was very, very sleepy. I resisted sedation, I was trying to keep awake.

My fear level was quite high. I was supposed to be in an ambulance. It was not a nice ambulance but a paddy wagon with bars like for prisoners. I could not talk to the driver. There were two benches on each side, and there was no gurney there. It was not an ambulance. The door had bars and so did the window.

Sedation overcame me. I was so sleepy sitting there. Thank God for Barney, who said, "I will accompany you. Don't worry, I will accompany you." That made me feel better. I sat on the other side. As best I could I kept awake, looking out the window and trying to figure out where I was being taken.

Finally we arrived at the mental hospital. Even in my dazed state at that time, I could think and was scared. I was really feeling alone in the USA, but my faith in God persisted. God was about to teach me another lesson in His Boot Camp.

CUCKOO'S NEST

"We are here now. It's a nice place." Barney said. And I looked. I was very sleepy with sedation, but I looked. It was a hospital all right, not the fearful whorehouse my mind thought they were taking me to. So I went in there. They admitted me to a room, a closed room. I just slept, slept, slept, and they gave me medicine. I tried to put the medicine under my tongue, or somewhere else, so I would not have to swallow it.

The nurses were very smart. They checked. They had a flashlight to check to see if I swallowed. I had to swallow. I slept most of the time. Finally I woke up the next day. I saw people sitting in front of the TV.

I said to myself, "I flew into the cuckoo's nest!" No really, it reminded me of that movie. That is real, to me, because I flew into the cuckoo's nest myself. I didn't want to, but I saw myself in that situation. I said that all these people had lost self-determination because of the effects of the medication. They were watching TV but not comprehending, just blankly staring with their heads shaking constantly, likely medication side effects.

Upon awakening, I had to go to the bathroom. The nurse asked for a urine specimen. When I opened the door, the aide was looking down. I don't know what she was looking at. I gave her the container.

I was sleeping most of the time. It was a nightmare! Then they cut down my dose of medicine, and my reaction was less. We had group therapy and I would sing for them. One day I went to the nursing station. My curiosity to know what was happening was great. There I saw my chart. On the front of my chart it said "suicidal."

"What is this?!" I told the nurse, "I'm not suicidal. That's my chart, but I'm not suicidal, I tell you." I was upset. Before that, a nurse's aide was required to accompany me on the grounds.

Certainly I was worried because my sister Bella was supposed to come visit me in Philadelphia. I told the aide, "She's coming to the United States to see me, but I don't know where she is. She's supposed to come but I'm here in this hospital. She doesn't know I am here. I hope she's okay."

It was several days before the first time I saw a psychiatrist. He asked me if I was interested in my director. I said, "Why would I be interested in him, that fat, ugly old man, when there are many young men around?" That's what I said. The doctor didn't ask me more than that. I told them I was not suicidal. I guess you have to be suicidal to be admitted. But I told them I wasn't suicidal. I told them I should not have been admitted in the first place. I got discharged that day. I must have been hospitalized there almost a week.

I was not able to write my family in the Philippines about this event. I could only think of my own situation. Besides, I did not even know what hospital I was at or its address. Years later, I discovered it was Friends Hospital in Pennsylvania. Historically this was the first privately run mental hospital in America and was founded by the Quakers. It was an hour or more from central Philadelphia. The core treatment offered by Benjamin Rush, MD, a Father of American Psychiatry, a signer of the Declaration of Independence and of Quaker lineage, was called "humane treatment" according to our psychiatric history lectures. I'm sure my care there did not measure up.

And that is what happened to me when I got sent to the cuckoo's nest.

STILL ALIVE

At least I was still alive after landing in the cuckoo's nest.

After my discharge from Friend's Hospital, I received a letter from Thomas Jefferson University that said I had to leave my apartment. I had one week to leave because I was not a part of them anymore, they informed me.

I had to grapple with reality. God and me. God is good, all the time. Actually God blessed me immediately for being hospitable. Filipinos are the most hospitable people on earth, they say. I remembered a month before that, a young woman named Phoebe Odom asked if she could stay with me. She was the daughter of a Baptist minister from Georgia named Sydney Odom. The Crowfoots, the Christian family I had stayed with in Atlanta when I took my solo trip to Disney World, had given Phoebe my number. For eternal reasons, she connected with me, asking if she could stay in my place for one week because she was going to attend the Bill Gothard seminar called "Basic Youth Conflicts." She was so excited about the seminar.

"Yes," I told her, "I have two beds in my apartment. You can stay with me free while you're in Philadelphia." So I had her in my apartment at that time.

Phoebe said, "Oh, I wish you could attend the Basic Youth Conflicts seminar." But I told her I was a resident, I couldn't just take off. But I got interested in it, that seminar that Gothard taught. He conducted these in major arenas all over the United States. It was very popular in the 1970s. The year now was 1972. After one week, Phoebe went back home to Georgia.

God prompted her remembrance now in my time of distress. Phoebe said she was coming back to Philadelphia to study music, so she could sing soprano. Her goal was to sing and perform on New York's Broadway. She came back to study ministry and take voice lessons.

How perfect is God's timing. She told me she was back

to Philadelphia in one month. That is just when my distress was happening! I called her up and said, "Phoebe, I'm in trouble. I stopped my residency because I felt like I was overwhelmed."

After my hospitalization I felt like I could not go back to my residency. I talked to my director and told him I wanted to stop. This is the same old man who said, "Come here," while knocking his knees together. Intentionally or not, he scared me. Actually he was very nice. I don't know why he did that. But anyway, I told him I was not finishing my residency, I wanted to stop.

He said, "Well, you have to go to human resources and sign out, tell them that you are stopping."

No problem with me. I was stopping. My director offered, "Why don't you go home first and rest, and then you come back? I'll get you back into residency." But human nature is such, when things like my experience happen, nobody wants to go back. In my mind I was not going back.

So I called Phoebe. By the grace of God, Phoebe said, "You know you can stay with me until you know what you want to do."

Thus, I give thanks for another episode of trusting God.

GOOD AND BAD

Now that Phoebe had said yes to my request for shelter, I spent the day packing. By design I left Thomas Jefferson University about 6:00 or 7:00 at night. I did not want people seeing me packing and leaving. It was my pride. I had very little to take with me really, just an ironing board and iron for my clothes, a suitcase and my guitar.

I hailed a taxi. A taxi with a white driver came by. When he got out of his car he looked at me. "What are you? Nigger?" And then he drove off, leaving me standing there. I was already feeling bad and now I felt terrible.

Immediately without my hailing another taxi, another one stopped in front of me. This time it was a black man driving.

I didn't know what discrimination was until I came to the United States. I didn't know anything about those things in the Philippines. However, now I know some of what the black people feel. Discrimination makes you feel like you're nothing, like you don't matter. But you still live a life, you have to live one.

Still I believe Americans are basically good people. I have been helped by Americans of all races. They were very wonderful. So, this white taxicab driver just proved a lesson from God's Boot Camp: there are two kinds of people anywhere in the world—the good people and the bad people. No matter what people they are, Americans, Filipinos, whatever, they are the same. There are the good ones and the bad ones. That black man was very nice.

When I look back on this experience now, I wonder if he was an angel from God. I didn't even call, he just stopped in front of me and said, "Do you need a ride?" I said yes. What else could I say? He put my stuff into the car, and I told him the address of Phoebe's place. I didn't know how to get there, but I just gave him the address. He knew where to take me.

He was very nice all the way while I was sitting in the back seat quietly. He was talking about the moon, the harvest moon that night, telling me how nice it was. "What a lovely evening it is." He was kind of cheering me up. I was very quiet, but my soul was comforted by this man who was very, very nice. It was taking the bad feeling out of me.

When we reached the apartment, he said, "Do you want me to help you bring your things upstairs?" The apartment was on the second floor.

I said, "No, no, just leave it here." Because it was not my house, I said, "Just leave it here and I will take it up." I paid him and he drove off.

Phoebe welcomed me. She let me sleep on her couch. Feeling God had protected me, I said a prayer of gratitude. In spite of hardship, I meditated on my great adventure coming to America. What if I had settled for a suitor who promised a golden cage and millions and millions? I would not be growing stronger daily through the freedom of opportunity. Finally, I prayed for the safety of my family in the Philippines under martial law.

THE GRACE OF GOD

What a blessing from God to reconnect with Phoebe. She was kind to give me shelter in Philadelphia after I left my residency.

Matthew 25:40 came to mind as Phoebe challenged me to help a woman who was mentally disturbed: "And the King shall answer and say unto them, Verily I say unto you, Inasmuch as ye have done it unto one of the least of these my brethren, ye have done it unto me."

Phoebe added, "But she won't go to a psychiatrist. Can you help?" Well, I'm usually very helpful by nature, even if I have my troubles. So I forgot all about my troubles. I thought it was just a bad incident in my life anyway. Now I had to live, had to go forward. I said I would be glad to help.

She said, "There will be a couple who will come this time tomorrow, about 6 or 7. I'll be in school, but they'll come to pick you up." I was very trusting. It was Phoebe who asked me, so I thought it was okay.

The next day this couple came to pick me up. It was a man and a woman, maybe middle-aged. They were in the front of the car, so I jumped in the back. I just sat in the back of the car and we drove on forever. I didn't say anything, because I was just wondering where we were going. Then we stopped in an old place in Philadelphia. I don't know where it was, because we drove maybe one hour.

Probably I should have asked about the location ahead of time. I thought it was nearby. There were houses everywhere, two-story houses, like row houses, but old. And there was no traffic, no traffic at all. It was nighttime, nothing was open. Everywhere was dark and quiet.

Suddenly a prompting of my spirit was alerting me to possible danger. Who were these people anyway? They parked in the middle of the area. Across the way was a warehouse. It was also dark. On the first floor of the building there were a lot of men, all making noise.

Now I was scared. I didn't want to get out of the car. Oh my goodness, who were these people? However, the couple got out of the car and said, "Do you want to stay?" I did not want to stay, as I was scared.

But I followed them, and they went into this place next door. I didn't even look where the men were because I was scared. It was a bar of some sort. Then there was a little landing and steps going up to the second floor. There was one light hanging there, maybe a 25-watt light. It was really dark. I noticed a door at the back. I thought maybe I would escape, because I was really scared to death. But to where would I escape? I looked around me. It was like a warehouse, open cabinets with boxes in them. My heart was pounding. I listened to all the noise from the men. I said to myself, "Oh no, I don't know what that is all about."

The fight, flight, or freeze autonomic nervous system response was kicking into high gear. I wanted to run away. I wanted to get out of the back door, but then where would I go from there? I didn't know where I was and there were a lot of men there. I didn't know where to go. Reasoning as best I could, I concluded that I was safer with these two people who were upstairs already.

My sensory capacity increased as I listened for any noise. I promised them in Jesus' Name that I would help. "God, I don't know what I am going to do. If somebody is waiting for me there, I don't know what I will do. I may go crazy or someone may kill me. But just be with me. I don't know what will happen to me, but I am in Your hands now."

So I tiptoed slowly and went up the stairs to the second floor. I look around. I saw the couple standing in one corner of the darkness. There were no other men. I was so relieved. You know the "peace that passes understanding"? I really had that at that time. That's the very moment that I had peace that passes understanding.

My eyes adjusted to the dimly lit room. A woman sat to my right side, in the corner on a sofa. I forgot all about my fear. I noted that all the windows had bars, and this woman was sitting there alone. She was sitting, and there was a coffee table and across that was an empty chair.

So I went to her. I was filled with compassion. I felt sorry for this woman and her distress. Her name was Louise. I sat down in that chair in front of her and said, "Louise, I'm Dr. Ganan. I work for Thomas Jefferson Hospital." I didn't tell her I actually was not there anymore. I said, "I am here to help you. I will accompany you."

I forgot all about myself; I was more interested in helping someone else. My role as a doctor and a Christian gave me courage. Louise was a white woman, probably middle-aged, and she was very quiet.

My role was to convince her to seek help. Ironically, I was asking her to enter a healthcare system that had been callous and uncaring to me. I asked her if her parents knew where she was. She didn't answer, she didn't say anything.

I said, "Do you know how long you've been here?"

She didn't answer.

I was thinking she was just a crazy woman, you know? So I said, "Well, Louise, I could help you go to the emergency room. I can accompany you."

But she still didn't answer me.

So finally, with the love of Jesus in my heart, I asked her, "Do you know Jesus?" That's what I asked her.

She didn't answer that either.

"Do you want me to pray for you?"

She nodded her head.

I don't remember the exact words I said, but I prayed. "You know Jesus, He is my Lord and my Savior." That's what I told her. "He is my Lord and my Savior."

But she didn't answer that, so I said, "I want to pray for you." I prayed that God would release her from the bonds of suffering.

I continued in prayer, asking God for freedom from anguish and fear. I placed her in God's hands. "Only Jesus can set you free." That's what I told her, which is true. "Only Jesus can set you free."

Amazing Grace! Now I look back, maybe what I meant was "set ME free," not just HER but ME! I don't know, but I just said those words. Here I was, blessed to be a blessing, through the providence of God putting the words in my mouth. I said, "Only Jesus can set you free."

She didn't say anything. She didn't budge, she didn't say one word.

After peaceful moments sharing our silence together, I stood up and looked up at the couple. They didn't say anything either. They just went down the steps. I followed them. I went down to the car, and they didn't say anything. They just let me off at my apartment, and that's it. That's the last time I saw them. I don't know what happened to Louise afterward. I had more events unfolding in my life to face and that event was soon forgotten.

Why did it happen? Was it part of being in God's Boot Camp? I now realize a lesson one must learn is obedience, no matter what. I believe now, it is a process of trust in God and knowing Him more. Yes, God is real! Indeed, He is!

Now I know in God's Boot Camp, this was the day of my healing. There but for the Grace of God go I! Maybe I could have been locked up forever. When I prayed, "Only Jesus can set you free," I probably freed myself.

"Fear thou not; for I am with thee: be not dismayed; for I am thy God: I will strengthen thee; yea, I will help thee; yea, I will uphold thee with the right hand of my righteousness." —Isaiah 41:10

BASIC YOUTH CONFLICTS

"Why don't you attend the 'Basic Youth Conflicts' seminar in Georgia?" Phoebe suggested with enthusiasm when she heard my story. "I know where you can stay in Atlanta, Georgia. They will have a seminar in October. Why don't you go and stay with the Crowfoots?"

Now I could go to Atlanta and attend Bill Gothard's seminar on "Basic Youth Conflicts" based on Christian principles. I went and was truly blessed.

Several years ago, the Crowfoots had been missionaries to India for more than ten years. After they returned to the USA, they reached out to international students. Their home was open as a non-denominational ministry.

At the final judgment God will only ask, "Do you know me? Do you love me? Have you obeyed me?" That's the main thing, knowing Him. The Americans make a big deal out of denominations. I have been educated in this matter now. God loves everyone! In any denomination or independent church, some people are mature and some immature; some go for selfish reasons to plead with God and some for true worship reasons just to praise the Lord. That's one more thing I have observed about life, now that I'm in God's Boot Camp.

So we called the Crowfoots in Atlanta. I talked with them and they agreed to give me food and shelter. I had some money left for the bus. Public transportation is common in the Philippines, thus I felt comfortable to ride the bus.

I stayed with Carris and Colin Crowfoot and their three sons. Every afternoon the youngest one, Peter, would take a walk with me. I think maybe his parents prompted him to do so. The Crowfoots accepted me for who I was. That comforted me. They put me in their home; they didn't question me, they just loved me. They didn't even charge me anything. I stayed with them three weeks. I tried to help as much as I could. I helped with the cooking and washing the dishes. It was all I could do. I didn't have any money, I didn't have a job.

(Recently I learned they were still alive, and I visited them. I told them my story of being briefly sent to the mental hospital during my residency. They just listened, nothing said, just listened. I told Mrs. Crowfoot, "I think they drugged me." She just closed her eyes. She was feeling my pain. I had thought I was drugged to begin with, because I am usually very brave. I am not a person who usually gets scared of anything. I am usually brave to say what I feel and think.)

What an adventure to attend the "Basic Youth Conflicts" seminar. With limited money for attending the meetings, somebody paid the $50 for a scholarship for me. What a blessing. I felt like I was with the Americans I dreamed of when I set my mark on coming to the USA. I was really very happy.

I learned a lot about conflicts youth have in life. Also, as a Christian I found answers to the conflicts that I had experienced in my great cultural awakening. I learned a lot. I have much gratitude for the kindness of the Crowfoots as well as other Christians. In fact, the Stonestreet family of West Virginia entered my life in Georgia. They were staying there to take their daughter to a Christian psychologist in Atlanta. They "adopted" me when I later came to West Virginia. Not to get ahead of myself, but years later, Mr. Denzil Stonestreet eventually stood in for my father, giving me away at my wedding to Greenbrier.

Their son, Greg Stonestreet, now a family practice physician, used to tell me, "God disciplines those He loves." I wondered at such a statement and actually somewhat quietly resented it. Many wrong events were going on in my life that they did not know. Why should I be disciplined? Did I do bad things? I thought I was not that bad, although definitely not perfect. I can only smile at those thoughts now. I understood only partly, looking at a dim mirror.

What I observed at the Basic Youth Conflicts seminar was that the American Christians worked well together. My preference was for the Baptists for being so good to me and helping me to grow more. So I learned a lot. (Greenbrier and I were married by an Independent Baptist minister. Yearly we go to Billy Graham's The Cove, a Bible training facility. Rev. Graham's roots are in the Southern Baptist Church. We meet international medical missionaries who come for a "Prescription for Renewal" weekend. They speak of God's work in medical missions performed by Christians of many denominations. My faith grows year by year. Meeting giants in faith helps me see how God can use me. On one occasion, I met author and pastor David Jeremiah in person. He is such a deep thinker and good teacher. These are people God is using in a mighty way.)

In Atlanta, God used the spark inside me, growing the fire. This explains how I grew during Gothard's seminar. A young Christian catches the possibility of Kingdom building for God.

During the seminar, a middle-aged male sitting behind me asked, "Are you enjoying the program?"

"Yes," I said, "I'm enjoying it very much." He was a stranger but I suspect a Christian like I. Because of his kindness I say God bless him. Somebody paid my way. God bless that person, too.

Definitely this time so alone in the United States was part of my boot camp experience. I found myself only with God. When God isolates you from everything, He can talk to you better. I lost my residency, so maybe God was calling me to ministry, I wondered. Details and plans worked smoothly for me to attend the seminar. This reinforced my Christian faith in a miraculous way. How inspiring! I see God's hands in all that was happening.

FINDING MY WAY
IN
TEXAS AND BELIZE

FREEDOM

How fortunate that my sister Bella did not come to Philadelphia like we initially planned. She found a nursing position in Dallas, Texas, before coming to United States. While staying with the Crowfoots, I received a letter from my mother telling me where my sister was and how to contact her. By the time I called her, she had her apartment. "Come on over, stay with me," Bella urged. So I rode the Greyhound bus from Atlanta, Georgia, after staying three weeks with the Crowfoots.

In Texas, every day I prayed, "God, what do You want me to do? I lost my residency. What do You want me to do?" I was really seeking God's direction in my life. And He answered my prayer. Bella worked at the Dallas Osteopathic Hospital. Other Filipino nurses worked there also. I think they all probably applied through some agency looking for nurses. God knew my heart. I was basically young and full of energy. I should work. I did not come to America to be dependent. I came to America to be independent. For freedom, I came. "Land of the free and home of the brave." I was brave. Free? I wasn't really sure about that.

Faith requires taking steps into the unknown but still holding God's hand. A nurse in the hospital knew of my predicament. She suggested I become a phlebotomist. I was a doctor and was good at getting veins, so why not, I reasoned. I was willing to do any job, any job at all. I didn't want to be dependent. I didn't come to be a burden to the United States, to the American people. I came here to help instead of being a burden. So I have prided myself. I wanted to work, to earn an honest living.

The baby step of faith became a major breakthrough. Yes, I would wake up at 4:00 in the morning to be there and draw blood. I was willing to do that. I applied and set up an interview.

In the perfect timing of God, an American nurse suggested to me, "Since you're a doctor, why don't you call this doctor?" She put his name and number down. "He's a good guy. He might be able to help you." So I had his name in my purse, then I was going for an interview to be a phlebotomist at 1:00 p.m. Imagine, there I was at the hospital, waiting my turn to interview. Meanwhile, as I was waiting, the Holy Spirit reminded me that I had this doctor's name. "Maybe I should call him first," I thought. My eyes spied the telephone at the nurses' station.

When I called he said, "Oh, I need help. Can I see you now?" What joy!

I left the hospital just before my interview, going back to my sister's apartment where Dr. James Krafft said he would meet me.

"My wife just died and I need help in my pediatrics office."

God is so good all the time. Dr. Krafft was the president of the Christian Medical and Dental Society. He was in the prime years of his practice and was around 50 years old. He had married a Mexican wife and he had two teenage kids. At this moment God knew the good doctor did need help.

From my heart, I'm telling a secret of mine: I was actually praying, "God, why did You have me meet this Christian doctor?" I wondered if he was the man God had for me. I knew my parents would question my wisdom (I questioned it too) since Dr. Krafft was about 20 years older with two teenagers! (Remember I had told God during my internship that I was willing to marry a widower. But I was not willing to marry someone who was divorced, no matter the reason.)

As I write my story, I get excited to convey how God has placed a shield of protection around me. Not only that, but He has blessed me in the midst of trouble. My sister Bella came to America, following her big sister. She settled in Dallas even as I received a letter from my mother mailed initially to Philadelphia but then forwarded to Atlanta, where I was staying with the Crowfoots. I was puzzled by how the letter got to my Atlanta address. Only Phoebe Odom knew where I went, and the hospital people did not know Phoebe, either. Life goes on and one cannot dwell on such puzzles. So for me, I went on.

The Crowfoot Family took me in at a crucial time in my life. They just loved me and further protected me. At that time I was seeking freedom and independence so much that I even considered maybe working as a restaurant waitress. Mrs. Crowfoot said, "No, don't do that. Stay with us, don't work at that. Men will make passes at you." That's what she said. I listened to her wise counsel.

As a teenager I did not want to sing the song "I Surrender All." The song scared me. Imagine, no control of yourself. I finally surrendered everything in God's Boot Camp. I learned complete surrender to God, my Father and King through His Son Jesus Christ, my Lord and Savior. I learned true Freedom in Jesus by giving all my cares to Him.

> I surrender all
> I surrender all
> All to Jesus, I surrender
> I surrender all.

> All to Jesus I surrender;
> All to Him I freely give;
> I will ever love and trust Him,
> In His presence daily live!

Why did I fear the singing and ultimately pledging all to Jesus? It was the best decision I have made.

GOD IS WATCHING

I sing because I'm happy,
I sing because I'm free,
For His eye is on the sparrow,
And I know He watches me.

—from the hymn "His Eye Is on the Sparrow"

This is the refrain from one of my favorite gospel songs. I lived through God's Boot Camp. He kept me under His protective eye.

God did not come to give us bad times. He planned for us good times, a good life. The refrain from this song is true—this I know. I heard about how good God is from the American missionaries. I surrendered all to Jesus. I'm in God's hands, I'm in good hands. I always believe that I must believe completely or not at all. It's an all-or-nothing type of thing for me.

When I lost my residency, I thought maybe God had something else for me to do. There was the opportunity for me to apply for a job as a phlebotomist. So I said, "God, if You want me to be a phlebotomist, I will do it. I have to wake up at 4:00 in the morning. I don't want to wake up at 4:00. I don't want to be a phlebotomist, but if that's the only job You have for me, that's okay. I'll take it."

Then miraculously this blessing came up. I met Dr. James Krafft and I took the job he offered. What a good mentoring position for a future pediatrician. I was examining newborn babies and his other patients daily.

Why should I feel discouraged,
Why should the shadows come,
Why should my heart be lonely,
And long for heav'n and home,
When Jesus is my portion?

77

My constant Friend is He:
His eye is on the sparrow,
And I know He watches me;
His eye is on the sparrow,
And I know He watches me.

If I may be presumptuous in declaring, God was blessing Dr. Krafft, too. His wife died, which was tragic, but he had helpers like Rosie and me. Rosie, his Mexican mother-in-law, became my friend. We liked each other.

Dr. Krafft did not know this, but actually I prayed, "God, maybe You sent me this man. He is a Christian man, maybe he is the one for me. That's okay, I'll take care of him." But he was old, I didn't want an old man! He was probably 50, and at that time I was in my 20s. Why should I meet this guy when his wife just died? But I would take care of him. I thought, "What am I going to do with two teenagers? That's a lot of trouble for me!" Still, I was willing, if that was God's will for me.

But nothing like that ended up happening. He did invite me to join the Christian Medical and Dental Society. He paid for my membership. He opened all sorts of doors for Christian service. One day, he wanted to show me something in his office.

There was a brochure there for *Amigos Internationales*, a medical mission going to Belize in Central America. Because of my medical mission training, I already had in my mind that I wanted to be a missionary, or learn more about medical missions. I said "Oh, I wish I could go." I told Dr. Krafft, "I would like to go volunteer but I don't have the money to go."

The costs looked way out of my reach: the airline ticket to Belize plus the expense of being a self-sufficient volunteer. Really all I had was the time, since I didn't have a residency position. Of course, I had a willing heart for missions.

Then later on, Dr. Krafft said, "I expect to hear soon whether you can go or not. I'll let you know." Three days later I got a note from him that I could go. What a blessing from God.

As Dr. Krafft's full-time assistant, I helped him check the babies in the hospital where he practiced pediatrics. He gave me a wealth of experience, though I was not paid in dollars. In prayer I asked God if He wanted me to be in pediatrics, because of Dr. Krafft.

And I was willing to accept the widowed Dr. Krafft as God's choice for me, if indeed he was. Coming from the Philippines where there is no legal divorce, I determined in my mind that I was not going to marry someone who was divorced. If a man was divorced, he was out of the picture for me. I didn't want to commit adultery. The Bible is clear about that, you make the person commit adultery, because they are divorced; whether the reason is good or bad, it's the same to me. I could only marry somebody who had never been married or was widowed.

God certainly watched over me in Texas day by day. In turn, I wanted to be in the center of His will. Be it the choosing of my professional career or marriage partner, I remained willing, knowing God knows best.

GOING SOUTH OF THE BORDER

Nothing is simple in this life. I am an American and a Filipino. I had a permanent visa. I told Dr. Krafft that if *Amigos Internationales* approved, I'd love to go on a mission. He inquired on my behalf.

"Yes," said Jim, the head of the group. Jim (I don't remember his last name), Dr. Echols (a family practice doctor from Texas, likely in his 50s), and a young dentist and his wife let me join them. I thought it would be a large group going, but there were only five of us.

So we went down to Central America. Thinking like a Filipino, I thought maybe in the mission field I'd need a knife. So I brought this fishing knife I thought may come in handy. I brought my guitar, and my transistor radio, too. I was not hiding anything. The pilot said, "Can I keep your knife with me?" Okay, no problem. So he kept it and returned it upon disembarking. When I got my guitar back, I saw that they had forced open the guitar case. I felt bad but realized they might have thought I was hiding something inside the guitar. I was not told that at the time, but that's what I thought. In God's Boot Camp and subsequently in His Army, I have come to expect battle scars. The guitar case still has a scar there.

Belize was our destination. We had to go to a place which is way down south called Punta Gorda. It is on the border between Belize and Nicaragua. How blessed I was to be a good hiker. We five hiked a lot. One day in the middle of the mission, they said we were going to another place where we had to ride a horse, as there was not much of a road. It was kind of a tough place.

God was training me. I volunteered, I was willing to do anything. I came from a third-world country. I knew what it was to be in a third-world country. So I was ready for anything. If I had to ride a horse, I would try riding. A Christian paid for my fare to go down there. I didn't want to disappoint that person or God.

Transportation was much like in the Philippines. One day to get to that day's destination, we had to ride a boat. Dr. Echols, Jim, a local man who was monitoring the boat, and I traveled together. I was the only female. I was wearing my long shorts, but still my knees were showing. I'm conservative, and I kept pulling my shorts and covering my knees when in the boat. They were missionaries, but still they were men and I the only female. The couple, the dentist and his wife, were not going that day. So I left them my radio, as they were interested in it. It was a transistor radio and they could listen to music.

Up the river at five-knots-per-hour we traveled. I kept taking pictures. I was interested in the scenery. Finally we reached a very remote area. We didn't do any medical mission. They just brought me along with them. They were talking to somebody about planning the mission. I was just taking pictures of the houses, the huts, the pigs, and the other animals there. I was curious.

God has given me training experiences that were not exactly answers to the prayers that I had requested. But through it all I've learned to trust in Him. "Lord, we don't need to know the reason our prayers sometimes go unanswered. Help us just to wait for Your time, because You are good." This is the prayer I offer as I reflect on my life journey from the third-world country of the Philippines to another third-world country of Belize.

MAROONED

A theme of my life is my knack of getting in a tight spot but then being provided a miraculous escape, thanks to God. In Belize, my dark night in the jungle was a doozy. It was probably the scariest night of my life.

The tide was against us, so we were trapped in an estuary at the mouth of the jungle river. A giant sandbar blocked our exit, leaving us in brackish water as the sun set. What could we do?

What did I sign on for, me, just a South Pacific Island lass? In boot camp the first thing a recruit learns is not to volunteer. But I had volunteered for this mission.

The mouth of the river into the ocean was blocked until the tide came in. Unless, like Moses at the parting of the Red Sea, we would experience a miracle. Our boat driver and navigator glided along the wide swampy river mouth, checking landmarks along the seashore.

We needed a safe place for the long night, protected from man and beast. What could I do? I volunteered, I was willing to go, but now we were marooned. I just prayed silently. I didn't say anything. Frankly, I was scared to death. Being Filipino, I knew too much about the jungle nights. My mother's stories of evacuation and hiding from the enemy in World War II came to mind.

Shelter lay ahead. We left our boat to hike into the darkening jungle. I just followed the group. We walked, looking for a place to stay for the night. I was thinking in my mind, "I can stay in a nipa hut of the very poor." I was thinking about maybe staying with a family, where I might lay my head. Would sleep come? And I was the lone female in the group. What should I do?

We couldn't go back. We were marooned. But what could I do, except to take things in stride? I was wearing my shorts. I had a decent blouse, but I was cold since it was night. It's not particularly cold there, but it was colder at night. At last they found an old abandoned unfinished medical clinic, and that was the place we would stay for the night. I wanted to go to the bathroom, so I told the group I had to pee. Jim said to go there in the bushes, so I went to the bushes. Scared of possible snakes and other scary bugs, but go I must! Luckily I remained safe in the darkness and rejoined the group. They had a kerosene lamp then which I assumed our local sea navigator got from somewhere.

Small blessing, the men had sandwiches and water to drink that they shared with me. We explored the abandoned clinic to use for the night. It was a two-story clinic. The first story had nothing finished, and the second story had two rooms. Probably one was to be an exam room, and it had room for a bathroom. There was a wooden bed there but no mattress or sheets and pillows. The room had a door but no lock either. The other room had no door at all, and no bed either. I was given the room with the door and the two American men the room with no door. The local man was to occupy the balcony in front of my room.

So I was thinking, "I can be brave and not complain, because I told God I'm going to go to Belize as a volunteer. All or none." The song "I Surrender All" came to mind. However, Jesus in the garden prayed for the cup of death to pass. I was scared to death, but I didn't say anything.

I was staying in the room with the door, but there was no lock. There was one bed there but there was no mattress, no pillow, nothing. What could I do? We looked for a bed sheet, but there was no bed sheet in the cupboard.

I inspected the construction of the room. In third-world countries, since it's hot, they often do not have solid walls up to the ceilings. They have the upper part made of banisters for air circulation, but in this building, some of the banisters were broken. I thought, "Oh no, the Americans might climb up!" I was scared of men. But they were Christians, they would not harm me, right? But they were men, and I was the only girl there. I was afraid of the

83

local guy too. My imagination went wild, but then by answered prayer, my soul became peaceful. I was in God's hands.

So the others were sleeping in the room with no door, and I would sleep in the room with the door that didn't lock. You know what? I was embarrassed to let them know I was scared of them. So I slowly pulled my bed, very, very slowly so they won't hear that I was moving things around. I put it against the door so at least nobody could come in.

Plan B crossed my mind, too. I was thinking about jumping out and finding another place to go. But it was dark and I didn't know where to go. I didn't even know where the path was. And if I went, I would go to a local person's house. I thought that could put me harm's way, too. I didn't know where to go anyway. I didn't know where we were.

So I was sitting on the hard wooden bed without a bed sheet. I said, "God, my parents don't know where I am now. My sister knows I have volunteered, but she doesn't know where I am. But You know where I am. Please take good care of me." That's all I said. I didn't want to sleep at all that night, I just wanted to keep awake to be alert. But I was too tired, and it was cold. I didn't have anything but a bed that had nothing on it, just a wooden bed, very, very hard. No pillow, nothing. It was cold. "Just take care of me." I was looking and hoping the other American men didn't climb over in the middle of the night.

I had to pee again in the night. I didn't want to go outside, since I had pushed the bed in front of the door. And the local man was sleeping on the balcony in front of my door. I didn't want to go there, I was scared. I didn't want the Americans to know I had to go to the bathroom, so I went in the corner where the bathroom was supposed to be. I peed right there, very, very slowly since I didn't want them to know. I didn't want to make noise! Anyway, eventually I fell asleep. Maybe I was too tired, even if I was cold. I prayed that God would take good care of me no matter what. "Whatever happens to me now, I'm in Your hands." So I just slept.

I woke up very early on my own. I pulled my bed away and looked for the local man, but he was gone. He must have gone to our boat to check things out. So I got out of my room and I saw the Americans sleeping on the floor with one white bed sheet over them.

I was very happy that nothing happened to me. When we went back, the sandbar wasn't there and we were able to get out. Hallelujah! No longer marooned!

DREAMS COME TRUE

I had a dream while serving as part of the *Amigos Internationales* mission in Belize.

Let me tell you the particulars about my dream, the before and after parts. I believe God gives us dreams for a reason. As this is my life in God's Boot Camp, I see reassurance from God in my dreams. My faith is small, so having a dream lets me see my way more clearly. Like the early Christians, I am a "follower of the Way"!

After only one week in Belize, the Americans said we had to go back to America. If I wanted to go back, I could go back with them. But I had promised God if He made a "way" for me to go on the mission trip, then I would volunteer. The deal was for one month, not one week. It would not be fair to the one who paid. I don't know who paid for my fare to go down there, but I used that money. It would not be right to go back after one week, even though I wanted to go back. I was tired. So I said no, I would stay for the term that I said I would stay.

So the Americans left. They took a small airplane to Belmopan, the new capital of Belize, to get the international flight. They left and I was at the airport when they left. Three days later, they put me with a Methodist missionary woman from England named Joan Moyle.

She accommodated me with open arms. What a blessing to work along beside her. A miraculous happening for me was the dream God gave me.

Every day I worked as a doctor in a mission clinic. Then in the evening I served as a guest speaker in local churches. Volunteering in God's Boot Camp can be exhausting. In fact, I got plumb tired. I was worn out. After three days, I said, "God, I'm really tired now. I want to go home now to the United States, but I will keep my word because I told You I was going to volunteer for one month. I should stay for one month. I don't want to go back

86

prematurely."

Our schedule remained nonstop every day like that. One night I dreamed. Before restful sleep I was praying and crying to God, "I want to obey You, but I'm really worn out and tired." Then God gave me a dream.

In the dream I went to a two-story nipa hut. It was so full of people waiting for me, I had to sit in the window sill with my guitar. Humbly I say that I am not a preacher, but God was allowing me just to share my faith with the people. I was singing, but again humbly I'm not a very good singer, but I can sing a little bit, so I sang.

There were two men in the dream, very prominent, watching me closely. They seemed to be very distinct. That was all of the dream. That's all I could remember, but the dream was vivid.

The next day, it was the same routine. I worked as a doctor during the day and at night I had to go someplace. I never knew where I was going, but they usually made arrangements for me to go. So I went. When they said, "Go there," I went there, because I had volunteered. So I went.

In the early evening we hiked to a place with a two-story nipa hut. It was so crowded, I sat on the windowsill. I told them of the love of Jesus. And you know, after it was over, I said, "Wow, that's the same place I dreamed about last night!" Exactly the same thing, except I did not see the two men from my dream watching me. I just put the dream in the back of my mind to ponder later.

Still, the very fact of dreaming something ahead of it actually happening made me feel energized, knowing God was with me on that trip.

Having grown in my faith, I now say my life is "Spirit led." My mind, body, and soul are all surrendered to God and His kingdom.

GOD AND LOVE

The two most difficult things to get straight are God and love. I am writing my memoir not because I have a clear understanding of God and love, but because I have learned in God's Boot Camp a thing or two that may keep another young lady who reads this from making a mess of her life.

What I have discovered is crystallized into a verse that I have repeated walking from exam room to exam room or hiking my beloved West Virginia hills. My little mantra goes like this: "Greater is He that is in you, than he that is in the world." This is a partial rendering of 1 John 4:4: "Ye are of God, little children, and have overcome them: because greater is he that is in you, than he that is in the world."

On my mission trip to Belize, when I was worn out I could say this and feel God's strength. When I had a swollen gum and needed a dentist, repeating this saying eased my suffering. When I needed a special lift, riding a four-seater airplane that came to pick me up at the airport, repeating my special verse then appeared to create favor. They put me in the front.

The pilot said, "When we are up in the air, do you want to push that? The plane goes down if you push it down. You pull up, it goes up." How exciting! I was so happy! I was in the front, plus I was excited to learn how to fly an airplane.

I had a layover in Belize City, as there was no seat for me on the airplane back to the United States. A Christian Belize family offered hospitality. God and love go together.

Then Dr. Krafft met me at the airport. He took me out to lunch. The mission dentist and his wife were there to meet us after the meal and welcome me back to the States.

"Greater is He that is in you, than he that is in the world." How blessed I am.

BLUE SKIES

I found myself humming a happy song one day as Dr. Krafft drove across the Texas countryside about two hours to an outpatient clinic where he doctored. As I rode along I noted there were no clouds in the sky. I was amazed, though I guess that happens. I said, "Where are the clouds? It's all blue." Then I said, "Where did the clouds go?"

Dr. Krafft started laughing, laughing at me. He said I was a breath of fresh air. "A breath of fresh air." He kept laughing. Well, with everything happening in our lives, we needed the release laughter brings.

Dr. Krafft led a Bible study in his home. He kept saying I was on the top of the ladder. I didn't know what ladder he was talking about, but I knew the song "We Are Climbing Jacob's Ladder," so his remark pleased me. I was "on the top of the ladder." In God's Boot Camp, where the growing in faith is rigorous, this pause refreshed me.

I continued my mentoring time with Dr. Krafft. Then he asked me where I wanted to go.

I said, "I don't know, because I don't know much about pediatric residency programs." He suggested seeking direction from the Bible as God's Holy Word. He directed me to Lamentations 3.

So I read Lamentations 3. I knew from the Christian missionaries that this book gives Biblical witness to the dignity of suffering by insisting that God enters into and is companion to our distress. Chapter 3 didn't speak anything to me, nothing. I did not question but remained puzzled.

Maybe Dr. Krafft wanted me to understand his suffering. Just like the Jewish people who celebrated their freedom from Egyptian slavery only to fall into Babylonian slavery, he had celebrated and enjoyed a good marriage with family but now suffered grief and loss. In fact, I read it again and again out of respect for the good doctor, but I did not know its meaning. It's all about Jeremiah lamenting the destruction of Jerusalem. But hope against hope is there because of God's great love:

> It is of the Lord's mercies that we are not consumed, because his compassions fail not. They are new every morning: great is thy faithfulness.
> —Lamentations 3:22-23

I didn't know where I wanted to go, but I applied locally, at least happy I knew Dr. Krafft because he could give me a good recommendation. But none of the hospitals in the local area accepted me.

Strangely, I got this call from a program I didn't even apply to, at the University of Michigan in Ann Arbor. In fact, I didn't even know the school existed. They called twice, to see if I'd like to go there for my residency. How did they know my number? How did they know I needed a place for residency? I was puzzled by this unsolicited offer. Besides, Michigan was too cold for me, and I knew no one there. So I declined the offer. Now I realize it's one of the best training places in the world. I just didn't know then.

Three years ago, I was reminded about this incident when visiting my daughter and her family in Ann Arbor. Maria had secured a dual position as both the student health psychiatrist at the University of Michigan and the psychiatrist with the oncology department at the University of Michigan Health System. She was living there since Justin Pope, her husband, who was with the AP as their national reporter for higher education, was selected for a coveted fellowship with the Knight-Wallace Fellowship Program for journalists. (The "Wallace" of Knight-Wallace is Mike Wallace, famous for his reporting on *60 Minutes*.) Justin is a summa cum laude graduate of Princeton University. He met my daughter at Oxford University in England. He was a scholar there, and my daughter studied there for a year as part of a program of Wellesley College, the premier college for women, before she went to Harvard Medical School.

So my decision making went on until I ended up in Charleston, West Virginia, where I got an acceptance. Two years in the Mountain State of West Virginia would be a good way to experience another environment, I reasoned. And I already knew some Americans there, the Stonestreet family. They were a great Christian family and "adopted" me and loved me. And unbeknownst to me, God had someone really special waiting for me to show up— Greenbrier Almond, my husband now. Praise the Lord. God provides in mysterious ways.

Also, I had heard about the Mountain State when at St. Margaret's Hospital in Pittsburgh. I thought I would like to go to "wild, wonderful West Virginia." I was dreaming of Baguio City in the Philippines, a summer resort for many as well as the Philippine Presidential Resort. Thanks to the Ganan Family connection through my brother, I had stayed in the summer resort of the Philippine Vice President, compliments of then-VP Lopez. When my brother had his honeymoon there, our family extended the celebration by tagging along. I was curious and awed by such a huge place. Those were the days. But I never liked politics. People are not sincerely your friends. My assessment is that many times they like you for your connections. How superficial!

Not me. I like being liked for just being me! God loves me as I am. How glad I am to be a child of a King, King Jesus! That's all I care about now. Oh how I sing "Great is Thy Faithfulness"! To God be the Glory! I am a child of a King! Jesus is my Lord! Hallelujah! Nothing could be better. Praise the Lord, praise the Lord!

WILD, WONDERFUL
WEST VIRGINIA

THE PLACE I BELONG

West Virginian by choice! From the beginning the fit has been comfortable. I felt the attraction of the mountains while in Pittsburgh studying and working as a medical intern. Later I got to know a family, the Stonestreets, who encouraged me so much. They welcomed me into their West Virginia home and took me to grand family gatherings on their farm. And now looking back through the eyes of faith, I realize God had someone there in West Virginia for me—Greenbrier!

The prompting of the Holy Spirit was strong. So I applied to the West Virginia University / Charleston Area Medical Center Pediatric Residency. I came down for the interview. Dr. Pomerance, the director, interviewed me. I was accepted, so I came to West Virginia, "Almost Heaven."

Calling back to thank Dr. Krafft for all his help, I told him, "Oh, my apartment is very nice. I look out the window and I see the forest."

He said, "Just like you. The forest, just like you."

Actually Tablas Island grows a tropical rain forest on its slopes, while West Virginia grows a temperate rain forest over 80% of its mountains.

He and I kept in touch for a while. When I met Greenbrier, I called Dr. Krafft and said, "There's a guy here. He is like you. He has a beard, and he's very skinny!"

He laughed.

"And he's a Christian, a very nice guy," I told him.

He laughed again. We didn't call each other anymore after that. I got busy with my life.

Initially my post-graduate residency proved very nice. Dr. Krafft knew that my director listened to my story of what happened when I was a resident, because I thought he should know. Dr. Pomerance listened, and he didn't say anything. He was nice to me.

In the middle of September, I decided I needed a car. I had my driver's license, an international driver's license. I didn't let it to expire. I wanted to have a car, too. It's hard to move in America without a car. So in September I decided I would go to the bank to borrow $5000 to buy a car. I went to the car lot. I wanted a hatchback. In America you can park anywhere, you even sleep in the car, so I wanted a hatchback. A Buick hatchback was only $4000, but that was a lot of money at that time. I borrowed $5000. Since I had a permanent job, I could put $200 down and then pay every month. They said since I had a job with the local hospital, it was fine. They approved it, and I got my car.

When my car was two days old, I called my sister in Dallas. I said, "Hey, I have a car now. Would you like to come and we'll go see the White House?" Another adventure awaited. . . .

AMERICA THE BEAUTIFUL

Upon returning from Belize, I was asked if I wanted to be interviewed on *Voice of America*. Nothing became of the offer, but I considered it an honor, as that radio broadcast beamed to the Philippines and many countries around the world, getting important messages out.

More vital to my life, I listened to the voice of God and decided on West Virginia for my pediatric residency. I knew the Stonestreet Family. I met them when I was in Atlanta attending the Basic Youth Conflicts seminar. Their daughter needed a Christian psychologist, and they had come there to meet with one. We stayed in the Crowfoot home together. They were a very nice Christian family. So I felt more comfortable coming to West Virginia. Blest be the tie that binds.

I was not thinking about staying in West Virginia long term. I was thinking I would spend two or three years in residency and experience the mountains. I wanted to see America, experience it. I'd been to the city, had a bad experience, so now I wanted to see the mountains. I'd heard about West Virginia, but just heard about it. I wanted to come.

My life was an open book. So I told my director about what happened when I was in residency, because I thought he should know. He was okay with it. God, the great "I AM," has taught me in His Boot Camp lessons that have guided my actions. Seeing the fall leaves of West Virginia reminded me of Moses and the burning bush. There Moses took off his shoes because he was standing on holy ground. Like Moses, I learned God is Holy, He will be with me in the dark times as light, and He will sustain me in my suffering.

Residency started well. I got my bearings, deciding by fall that I needed a car. My choice was a Buick hatchback, because in America you could park anywhere and use the back for sleeping. So I called my younger sister, now a nurse in Dallas. "Come on! Let's see the United States!"

Honestly I think I got into more trouble by driving directly to Washington, D.C. "Let's go see the White House first!" Interstate 79 had just opened. I looked at the map: "Oh, it's not too far away." I didn't know anything about driving! I could drive, and I was brave and young. I was 29 years old then. So we went to the White House. It was a new car and it still had a paper on the front. We didn't even take it away because the car was new. We didn't want the carpet to be messed up. I said, "This is the way to go, Route 50." Well, I didn't know the shortcuts at that time. I was new in America. I was just excited to have a car so I could see the United States.

So we went to Route 50. Because it was fall and the leaves were changing, we stopped somewhere at a roadside park along Route 50 and took pictures. My sister was wearing ladies step-in sandals. So anyway, we got back to the car after taking pictures outside. It was natural for her to leave her sandals outside, and we drove off. One hour later she said, "Where are my sandals!?"

So I started laughing and said, "We will just tell President Nixon that we came from West Virginia and we don't wear shoes!" Because that's the joke they have, and I had heard about it, that's why I said that. I was thinking that we could just stop off somewhere and buy something cheap to wear. But apparently she had extra shoes in her luggage.

We passed the sign that indicated the way to Arlington Cemetery. Well, it was already nighttime. I didn't want to go anywhere else now, so we drove on. I was so brave at that time. There wasn't as much traffic back then, and since it was nighttime, there wasn't a lot of traffic anyway. We went into downtown D.C. and we needed gas, so I stopped and we filled up. There was an attendant there, so I asked him, "Do you know where the White House is?" I don't know what time it was, probably already 10:00 or 11:00.

He was looking at me like I was crazy. Well, we had come to see the White House. We were just naïve. He didn't answer us. He just had a surprised look, like, "What are you trying to ask me?"

We drove off. We went around and around. It was already 11:00. We had a good time at the Washington Monument. We were the only people there, it was so late, maybe even midnight already. All the flags were around the monument. We were so excited to be there. We found the White House eventually. Then we passed a major hotel there by the White House. (In fact I stayed there one time years later for a medical meeting). We didn't have credit cards, and I'd never stayed in a hotel before in my life, even in the Philippines. In our culture we stayed with people, but not in hotels, especially the smaller hotels. It was mainly the bad people who went there, the bad women, you know? In the Philippines we stayed with families.

My, my. I had to pee. Another bathroom story! There was a bathroom but the gate was down. It was closed. It was midnight now, or at least late at night. I didn't know where to go, but I had to pee. So we parked by the Monument and opened the door and I sat down there. Today there would probably be a camera watching me!

Now to try out the benefit of a Buick hatchback. We had to find a place to bed down. So we parked, I don't know what street it was, but it was behind the White House. We parked there. I thought that was the safest place on earth to be, because the President needs protection, so there must be police there, we would not be harmed. So we parked there. We went to sleep.

Before I knew it, there was the sound of walkies-talkies and the light of a flashlight on us. I tell you, I was startled. I jumped up.

The policeman said, "Where is your driver's license?" I had no local driver's license, but I did have an international driver's license. I showed it to him. I don't know what he did with it, but he returned it to me.

I said, "Can we sleep here for the night?"

The man said, "Well, we change guards at 4:00. You have to go at 4:00, we have different guards then." Do you think I could sleep again after that? No! I was too excited. I was too nervous to sleep again. So I just sat in the front of the car there and waited for the time when we had to leave. God and my guardian angel have worked overtime protecting me. I thank Him every day. My lesson learned is like that of Dr. Moses ("doctor" because as Pharaoh's daughter's adopted son, he had the education of a physician). I know God is Holy. There are times to take off our shoes and go barefoot. And there are dark times, but God will help us find our way. Yes, there is suffering, but God comforts us.

SPIRITED DRIVE

What I write is the truth. My life experiences are sometimes scary and sometimes humorous, but they define me. My qualities formed by definitive events mixed with my nationality, my family teachings and my own youthful attitudes are important to my ethos, my drive, and indeed, my spirit.

On my first road trip in America, I had no concept of distance or time. Tablas Island, Philippines, has few roads and time is "Filipino time."

"Oh, Atlantic City is right there, not too far away," I exclaimed to my sister in the parked Buick hatchback near the White House in Washington, D.C.

So we drove to Atlantic City at the 4:00 am change of shift time for our friendly policeman, who had allowed us to park there behind the White House. We arrived in Atlantic City early in the morning before anyone woke up. We ate in one of the restaurants there, but we had to wait until they were open. I don't know what time it was, maybe 8:00 in the morning, when we walked the boardwalk alone by ourselves.

Then we had to go back to West Virginia. We had seen the White House already. So I told my sister, "We are going to stop by Pittsburgh, because that's where I interned. I can show you my hospital." So we drove to Pittsburgh. I didn't stop anywhere. My last gasoline fill-up was in D.C. By the time we reached Pittsburgh, I had maybe a quarter of a tank or something like that. I didn't even look at the gas gauge, actually.

We arrived at St. Margaret's Hospital at around 6:30 p.m. All the people I knew in the hospital had left for home, but Bella still got to see the place. After a brief tour, we left for West Virginia. My sister had a flight early in the morning on Sunday. She had come on Friday. We left Charleston about noontime on Friday, which is why we arrived in D.C. at nighttime. It was really crazy.

My pediatric residency was part of an expansion of West Virginia University School of Medicine in Morgantown with the Charleston Area Medical Center. We drove past Morgantown. It was already nighttime. My gas tank gauge read almost zero. I needed to find a gas station, but all the gas stations were closed. It was early in the morning already, past midnight. Now my lack of sleep on this road trip was catching up to me.

We were out of gas. I didn't tell my sister that I was scared. I knew we had to find gas, but I thought maybe we should go further along. My, my. The interstate was new at that time, so there were no places on I-79 to fill up. The fog shrouded us in the dark night. I couldn't see anything.

We stopped at a rest stop. However, there were big trucks lined up, and the male drivers were sleeping. I thought maybe we could sleep there, too, but I didn't want these men to see us girls, because we would be in danger. So we covered the windows. I still felt uneasy about it, so I thought I should drive on. So I did. But I never told my sister I was scared. The gas was on zero now. I didn't know where the next gas station was.

At one point I thought I saw two gas stations, but because it was foggy, I could not be sure. Maybe I could stop somewhere and knock on someone's door? But then I didn't want to do that, because I thought: "If I knock on someone's door early in the morning, I look like a stranger and they will be scared of me; I might get hurt." So I didn't do it. I said to myself, "I'll just go on."

Let me tell you, my prayers were constant and fervent. I drove on. I knew the car would stop anytime now. I was really feeling bad that I was endangering my own sister. She was just innocently riding with me, but she never got scared, because I never told her I had no more gas. It was a miracle we didn't run out of gas. I could see only two or three feet ahead of me because of the fog. We had to drive slowly because of that. In the early morning light once the fog lifted, we began to drive fast to make it to the airport.

I was new in the United States and wanted to help like an American would. Kindhearted by nature, I always wanted to help people. On our way to Charleston, we stopped when we saw a young man hitchhiking. This was a common means of transportation in the mid 1970s. (Later when I served as "Doc" to the veterans at the Clarksburg Veterans Affairs Medical Center, I heard thrilling stories of World War II veterans wearing their uniforms and thumbing across America. Sadly, the Vietnam combat vets had to take off their uniforms if they expected to catch a ride. America certainly had changed.)

On this early fall day, there was a young man on the roadside. He had a jacket over his left arm, and he was making the hitchhiking signal. I stopped there and said, "Do you need a ride?"

My sister transferred to the back, and he sat beside me in the front.

I said, "Where are you going?" He said he was going to visit his girlfriend who was a student at college.

So we drove off. He was very quiet. He just sat there, seemingly a very nice person. I was the one talking, asking him for directions. We exited I-79 and he said, "Here, you can let me off."

My mind drifted back to the Philippines and Sunday school lessons taught by the American missionaries. I prayed for this young man and his girlfriend as I was reminded of the verse: "Be not forgetful to entertain strangers: for thereby some have entertained angels unawares." (Hebrews 13:2)

What an adventure! God made a way when there was no way, and Bella made her flight. I believe she and I were protected by our guardian angels. When Jesus said He came that we might have life and have it more abundantly, He surely had this South Pacific Island girl in mind.

LOST IN TRANSLATION

Dr. Arthur Shawkey was one of my attending physicians during my residency. He was one of the attendings that I admired and respected the most. He must have been a Christian, though I don't know where he worshiped. He was a very nice man. One day he and his wife invited me to their home for dinner.

They took a personal interest in me. I was telling them a story from my youth about when my father took me to the market. I was in grade school, so I felt privileged that my father took me to the public market. We saw a huge sea creature. I think it was a giant sea tortoise. There were tears in his eyes and I thought the turtle was crying. I had a tender heart even in childhood. Boldly I asked my father if we could buy the creature and release it in the sea. It must have cost a lot. Being in the market the turtle must have been food to someone. I was telling them that story, and suddenly Dr. Shawkey said, "That's a big lie!" I didn't know what to say. I just kept quiet. I wanted to tell him it was not a lie, it was true.

Greenbrier told me later about idioms where the meaning is obscure. He used the example from psychiatric medical history. If a child says, "My father beat me up today so I could come and see you," this would not be child abuse. What the child is saying in idiom is that his father woke up extra early, earlier than the child, to milk the cow, feed the chickens and slop the hog so the chores were completed before the father and child had to drive to town to keep the doctor's appointment on time. No need to call child protective services!

So Greenbrier figures Dr. Shawkey was just exclaiming in awe about a fantastic story that he found heartwarming because of my compassion. But I didn't know what the "lie" was, so I did not know how to respond. Our communication was simply lost in translation.

SUICIDE NEVER

I trained to be a children's doctor because the Philippines has so many children. By coming to America, I trained against greater resistance than I would have back in the Philippine Islands. I trained to be strong mentally and morally with the elite of the educational ranks. I suspect a fair comparison would be training for service as a Navy SEAL.

Jesus trained the same way, as it is written. Isaiah tells us: "Surely he hath borne our griefs, and carried our sorrows: yet we did esteem him stricken, smitten of God, and afflicted. But he was wounded for our transgressions, he was bruised for our iniquities: the chastisement of our peace was upon him; and with his stripes we are healed." (Isaiah 53:4-5)

In the midst of my pediatric training, a Filipino doctor friend of mine called me up and said that a classmate of ours, another Filipino, committed suicide.

I said, "Why?"

She said, "Because she was depressed."

"Depressed about what?" I said.

I pondered how this could be. Her peace was so disturbed that a strong-willed Filipino woman, a doctor, a classmate, could give up after making it through medical school and then coming to America like I did. Why did this doctor commit suicide? Why would she take her own life?

With the help of Jesus who laid upon Himself "the chastisement of our peace," no matter what happens to us, we should never commit suicide. We serve a risen Savior and "with his stripes we are healed." Therefore, though shaken to the core by this suicide, we should never give up.

We continued our phone conversation, asking each other, "Why?"

Thank God for the teaching of the American missionaries who grounded me in Scripture. I shared that

Jesus redeemed us from the curse of the law, being made a curse for us (Galatians 3:13). He was made a sin-offering, and He died in our place, on our account, that He might bring us near to God. It was this, doubtless, which caused His intense sufferings.

My last thought before deep sleep was that Jesus experienced in that terrible hour a great suffering on the Cross endured by Him but due to us. As is my custom, I prayed, praising God Who can answer "why" questions. I thanked Jesus for His suffering by which, and by which alone, I was saved from eternal death. Then I thanked the Holy Spirit for the comfort of peace.

PER ARDUA AD ASTRA
"Through Adversity to the Stars"

My life follows the pattern of other soldiers who have gone through boot camp. This story's title is the motto for the British Royal Air Force. Here are some examples of the adversity I faced in my residency.

My director put me and us all to hard labor. Our pediatric program was in Charleston Memorial Hospital, which had about 4,000 deliveries a year. We attended many of these births by consult whenever fetal distress was an issue. Let me say, American women do not take as good care of themselves as Filipino women.

Our program had a very large pediatric intensive care unit. As a referral service to southern West Virginia, we saw the sickest of the sick babies. While I am grateful for the experience, I labored night and day with the critically ill newborns. Sometimes the results were heartbreaking. Other times we would save a life, but the baby would never be right neurologically or would be otherwise severely impaired.

Our emergency room served trauma and burns, and we had a pediatric ward with severely injured children. Sometimes this was accidental and sometimes from child abuse.

And we were on the cutting edge of medical science and practice at Charleston Area Medical Center, with West Virginia's first renal transplants and cardiac intensive care, just to mention two areas that I am now proud to have been part of.

I held onto God's truth as I worked so very hard. Before I went on mission to Belize, I had met with a pastor who counseled me with the Holy Scripture: "If ye continue in my word, then are ye my disciples indeed; And ye shall know the truth, and the truth shall make you free." (John 8:31-32) The pastor also said, "God is spirit, and we should worship Him in spirit and in truth," from John 4:24. I was puzzled and perplexed, as I had heard that verse before but didn't know why he was quoting it to me.

God's Boot Camp was filled with adversity; however, I did my work. But my director was so hard on me, really, really hard. Sometimes fellow laborers in the hospital could be unfair, too. I can remember that someone took my left arm and looked at it carefully, like checking for needle marks common in drug users. I've never used drugs in my life. One person commented, "The walls have ears."

I admit my strength to go on was stretched to the limit of my ability. Actually I said, "I'm smart enough to have ears, maybe they are following me."

Though I did not have major past sins, I did tell my director at the start of my residency about some of my troubles in my internship and previous residency. In those situations I rationalize that I acted in love and compassion. "Greater love has no man than this, that he should die for his friends." Those are Jesus Christ's words, but maybe the fact that I was the spokesperson of the interns at St. Margaret's Hospital in Pittsburgh caused me troubles. After all, I would not reveal who had started the petition complaining of inadequate supervision.

Being a Christian makes one a target of Satan's attacks. We are called to resist the devil. I choose to be one who does God's bidding, no matter what. That's my story and I'm sticking to it.

As a trained disciple of Christ, my final assignment in life is to bring God back into our midst and to urge us to turn from our wicked ways, to ask forgiveness for our disobedience. The time for the second coming of Jesus Christ, King of Kings, Lord of Lords, is not too far away. God is real. I look forward to one of those reward stars we pediatricians give to children when they take their medicine and eat their peas. His presence is our blessing.

Per ardua ad astra: through adversity to the stars.

HELPERS

> Look for the helpers. You will always find people
> who are helping.
>
> —Fred Rogers

My pediatric residency let me touch the lives of countless children who were growing up watching Public Broadcast System (PBS) TV, including *Mr. Roger's Neighborhood* and *Sesame Street*. I hardly had time to watch TV, but I knew the main players like Cookie Monster.

Then Christmas came. I felt blue. At Christmastime, we long for home. But someone must care for the sick. *Moi!* I was put to work because I was single, I didn't have anyone.

Friendship takes time to develop. I hardly had time to eat or sleep. I didn't have any friends except for two people. Carol Johnson, who was from Panama, lived in our house-staff apartment building. Carol was not a doctor; she was a nurse studying to be an anesthetist. Then there was the internal medicine resident, Dr. Hans Ruprecht, whose apartment was beside hers. We helped each other by sharing as friends.

We three were internationals. We were searching for friends and found each other. They were truly great friends. Hans was from Switzerland. He was very strange, but a very nice guy. He was a pilot. In fact, later on after Greenbrier and I were friends already, he invited me to be his first solo flight passenger. Well, I was excited to ride the airplane! So I said yes, and I invited Greenbrier to come along, but Greenbrier would not go. It was Hans's first solo flight, so Greenbrier didn't want to go. But I went. And we were up in the air, looking around. I was taking pictures. It was exciting.

My life story is about living on the edge. As we were flying, Hans said, "Oh, there is ice on our wing." I don't know how he knew there was ice. We had to land at another airport in West Virginia, not in the Charleston area, but at another airport in the middle part of the state. So we landed there. I'm thinking now, I didn't know much about airplanes. We walked around there, he waited for the ice to melt, then we went back. I was excited riding the airplane. One thing I wanted to do was learn to fly an airplane. (Greenbrier and I shared that dream to be pilots, but after marriage and having our children we narrowed our wishes, as we felt the risk-taking would be unfair to them. Parents think that way.)

Hans, Carol and I would gather in my apartment. I lived on the fourth floor, they lived on the first floor. I would invite them over. Hans would sing in foreign languages. He was European and knew a lot of languages. Carol was very nice. I don't know where she is now. For a while she was in California, but then we lost track of each other. Maybe God will open it up and we will see each other again.

So Christmas came, and I said to God, "How come the others have boyfriends and I don't have a boyfriend? Jesus is more than enough of a gift, but I want a Christmas gift this year—a boyfriend. You promised that the best and perfect gift comes from You. I want nothing less than that perfect gift, but if You meant me to stay single, I will accept it. But You know I want to get married, I want to have children, I want to have a family." That's what I told God. "But if You don't want me to marry, I'll just go home and be with my family."

Truly, God knows best. Before He brought Greenbrier and me together, he brought Carol and Hans into my life. We were helpers to one another. My lesson learned in God's Boot Camp is: Be patient, God is always on time.

JUST FRIENDS

Bill Harris became my friend in the fall of 1973 when he rotated through pediatrics from West Virginia University School of Medicine. Bill was a funny guy. He was loud. He was a good guy, just loud. He was a good Christian guy. One day he said, "Dr. Ganan, I want to show you West Virginia. I want to take you on a tour around West Virginia."

I believe his heart was pure. He knew I came from the Philippines. My idea was, I had heard this, if you go with these American men, you have to kiss them and you have to sleep with them. That terrified me. That was enough to scare me off! So I said, "Well, not me." So he left me alone.

After one month he was still there. I knew him better as a person. He was a nice guy. He paid this lonely Filipino a great compliment when he serenaded me West Virginia-style, playing his guitar and singing "The Most Beautiful Girl in the World." He brought his best friend with him which was also culturally correct as far as I was concerned.

Later on he came back alone. Again he said he would like to show me West Virginia. I trusted him now, so I went. We went everywhere, like to Twin Falls, and he took pictures of me. We went to a park where you could see the river. There was a train there also. He showed me all that.

He was from Fenwick, West Virginia. We drove over there through some beautiful mountains. He introduced me to his mom. She was a little startled, though I don't know why. All the family was there—grandparents, aunts and uncles. They were having a reunion.

Then coming back he said that he wanted to buy me coal jewelry, earrings. I didn't want anybody to buy me any jewelry. I felt embarrassed. I said "No, no, I don't want that." So we headed toward home. On the way home there was this big storm. It was already getting dark. I was getting scared. I was alone with this guy, and it was 6:30 in the evening now.

Thank God for His Word planted in my heart. In the midst of this West Virginia storm, I thought of the Filipino storm when we as children went to the movies, knowing our parents would not approve. Now Scripture came to mind:

"What doth the Lord require of thee, but to do justly, and to love mercy, and to walk humbly with thy God?" (Micah 6:8)

Bill stopped the car. I got scared. I was very quiet, because I was thinking about the storm. We were not too far now on our way back to Charleston. I was actually scared of a typhoon. He had to stop the car, as the rain was really bad, and the lighting and thunder were really bad.

Then he said, "Are you scared?" I just kept quiet. He said, "Don't be scared. We are in the safest place in the world. If there is any place to be in a storm, it's in a car when it's lightning." He said it was because of the rubber tires. I didn't know that before.

But my mind was thinking: "What do I do with this guy? He is taking me home. I don't know what to do with him. I live alone in my apartment, I don't want anybody there. I don't know what he will do."

My woman's intuition told me he was a nice guy, but I didn't know. I didn't really know him. I would not sleep with him for sure. I was really scared. I didn't know what to do with him. Should I invite him to my apartment? My prayer was to find a way to be gracious but not to compromise my vows of purity to God.

So I was already thinking about that. I was quiet because of that. When we reached the apartment, we had to ride the elevator. In the elevator I thought, "I will just say goodbye to him and shake his hand." That's what I did. I stopped by the door and said, "Thank you very much, Bill," and I shook his hand. We ended the evening as friends.

Later on, before he could tell me anything, I said, "Bill,

I think we will always be friends, the most wonderful friends all our lives." And you know, he was very unhappy. You could see the sour face. Maybe he liked me more than just a friend. But I knew in my heart that he would just be my friend. He never came back after that. I called him up and said, "Bill, how come you are not visiting me anymore?" Because I liked him.

But I did not know the American idiom, so my "just friends" remark was actually code for rejection to Bill, I can see now. He was nice, actually, and he was like a brother for me. He was a nice Christian guy, just not right for me romantically. He didn't come back, so I got lonely again.

When he returned to WVU upon completion of his rotations in Charleston, he caught up on all the news with Greenbrier, as they were friends. They were talking, and Bill mentioned me, that I was a beautiful girl and a virtuous woman.

Greenbrier asked, "Are you related to each other in a romantic way?" That's what Greenbrier later told me.

Bill laughed, recalling our parting at the apartment door. "No, we are just friends."

In anticipation of his own upcoming rotations in Charleston, Greenbrier questioned, "Is it alright if I meet her?"

Apparently Bill said it was okay, since we were just friends.

Unbeknownst to him, Bill helped set the stage for what would eventually become a great friendship and then romance and marriage for Greenbrier and me. God works in mysterious ways!

PHOTOGRAPHS

Araceli's graduation from
Far Eastern University School of Medicine in 1967

Araceli with her parents
Nemesio Fausto Ganan, Sr., and
Maria Villanueva Ganan
Far Eastern University School of Medicine graduation,
1967

Araceli on her wedding day
September 13, 1975

Almond Family at Greenbrier and Araceli's wedding
Ruth Almond Wiewiora (married to Rich), works for Cru®
(Campus Crusade for Christ®)
K Almond (married to Thom Keely), pastor
Greenbrier and Araceli, physician
Lois Flanagan Almond, mother
Harold David Almond, father and physician
Anne Almond (married to Richard Low), entrepreneur
(not pictured): Beth Almond Ford, historian/writer

Araceli, baby Maria, Greenbrier
1977

The Ganan Siblings, mid-1980s
at the garden of the Crystal Cathedral in California
L-R:
Lilia Serra (married to Ignacio), pharmacist
Nemesio Ganan, Jr. (married to Grady Ngo), attorney and
Filipino Assemblyman
Jesusa Villamor (married to Anacleto), banking and finance
Priscilla Aborka (married to Rio), dietitian
Araceli (married to Greenbrier), physician
Edna Ganan, administrative and executive assistant
Bella Ganan, nurse
Onedo Ganan (married to Mariles), engineer

Greenbrier, Roncevert, Araceli, Maria
Along the Maine sea coast
The children were at summer school at Harvard University.

Araceli touring Yellowstone National Park where she and Greenbrier vacationed as empty-nesters in the late-1990s.

Family Thanksgiving gathering, Durham, NC
L-R (top row 1ˢᵗ):
Roncevert David Ganan Almond, son. Attorney and
currently partner at The Wicks Group
Yasmine Landin Almond, daughter-in-law. Currently
executive assistant with Blue Origin
Maria Luisa Ganan Almond, daughter. Psychiatrist
Justin Pope, son-in-law. Currently chief of staff
at Longwood University.

Greenbrier and Araceli on a Mediterranean cruise

GREENBRIER:
THE DATING YEARS

ENCHANTING

Greenbrier came into my life in an enchanting way. He came down from West Virginia University in November 1973 for his rotations in radiology, obstetrics-gynecology, and emergency room. He was a fourth-year medical student. I was ahead of him, having graduated from Far Eastern University School of Medicine in 1967.

A Christian woman, a saint, gave me a book entitled *The Promises of God*. It was a compilation of promises from the Bible. I read that every day, every day, every day. I read every page of that book. I prayed to God, "Here in Genesis You said—and I agree with You—it is not good for man to be alone. Look, I am lonely. Nobody is taking care of me. I'm always in trouble and no one is defending me. I am an old maid now. I am ready for a boyfriend. I am not ready to marry but would like to meet the man I am supposed to marry, to have a boyfriend." I didn't want to get married yet, because I was not ready, even though I was already 29. I said, "I want to meet the guy You have for me. I told You, God, I would wait for the man You have for me. I want You to be my matchmaker. If You do not want me to be married, it is okay. But I want to get married and have kids." I told God that. Still nothing happened.

I can look back now and see that God answered my prayers. *The Promises of God* said that God looks into the hearts of men and women whose hearts are totally His. So I asked God, "Am I not Yours completely yet that You do not hear me? I want Your choice, not mine. You know me inside and out and know perfectly the one suited for me. Surely You have someone that is perfect for me." Greenbrier showed up at the perfect place and time.

When he came to CAMC, I thought he looked weird! He did look weird to me. He was very skinny, had blond curly hair down to his shoulders, and a long beard, too. He was hippie-looking, not my type. I liked a clean-cut guy.

126

That was my ideal. I didn't know Greenbrier personally, but I knew the names of the medical students when they came to the hospital. They paged us, so I knew his name, Dr. Greenbrier Almond. But he wasn't my friend, as we had not met formally. But he was actually probably already interested to know me, given his prior conversation with classmate and friend Bill Harris about me.

One Tuesday I was on call all night. It was a night of hard labor because they would call me, "Emergency room, ICU, and the pediatric floor," all at once. Where do you go first? So I didn't sleep at all that night. Every Wednesday we doctors had to go down to radiology to read x-rays. So that day I was very sleepy.

To this day I cannot explain what happened, except just to say God had His hand in our meeting. Maybe that is sufficient. I like the poetry from the musical *South Pacific*, which speaks of an "enchanted evening" whose explanation cannot be given by mere words. Greenbrier was there, since he was in his radiology rotation. I went down to the room a little bit later, and all the seats were full except for one available seat on the sofa. Greenbrier was seated on the sofa on one end, another doctor on the other side, so I asked them if I could sit between them. They said it was okay. It was a four-seater, so I sat between them. The lights were off so we could read the x-rays, our teacher explaining the pictures in the x-ray boxes. I was so sleepy, and my head kept dropping sideways and forward. I did not sleep the night before, as I had been on call. I was embarrassed. I was joking to Greenbrier. I said, "May I sleep on your shoulder?" No response; I thought I was not very funny or maybe I shook him up. Reflecting later, I could see that we met in a way only God in His love could plan.

Every time I remember our first encounter, I think that it was very funny. He didn't say anything, nothing. Nothing happened. But then, everything happened! What an enchanting moment.

A TIME AND SEASON FOR EVERYTHING

Definitely I experienced a turning point around Christmas 1973. Cold and lonely, Christmastime came. That Friday I took my on-call duty, sad to be alone but glad to be busy just to distract myself. Then I went to church on Sunday. The Bible Center Church, because it was just a small church, asked me to speak to the young people in another building. So I went there with my guitar.

Greenbrier had been home to Buckhannon for Christmas Day but caught a ride back to Charleston on Saturday. Now on Sunday he walked to my church. Everybody was welcoming him and asking where he worked.

He said, "I work at CAMC. I'm from WVU."

They said, "Oh, do you know Dr. Ganan?"

Greenbrier remembered the radiology round, us meeting. "Yeah, of course I know her. Where is she?"

Well, I wasn't there but with the children. So after the service, I went to the main sanctuary and the people said a student doctor named Greenbrier from CAMC had been in church but had left already.

I lingered with my church family that Sunday. Filipinos are wonderfully hospitable. Because of Christmas, which we celebrate all 12 days, I thought I would invite some of my church family to dinner. Dr. Wallace the church organist and his wife Clotile agreed to come. Tom Wallace and I shared a love for music. Fortunately for him, after his wife died and left two daughters to raise, Clotile married him. Through them I met the owner of the Bible bookshop in Charleston. They all agreed to come. The church sponsored a missionary to Brazil, Judith Gentry. Her mother, Miss Mary, was a retired missionary. They too accepted my invitation.

Another lesson in God's Boot Camp had been learning how to cook. What a challenge. In the Philippines, my mother always had helpers who cooked. My guests may not have realized that I was not a good cook. I had to learn how to cook, but I had watched our cooks. I told myself if I was smart enough to learn medicine, then I could learn how to cook. I called people up, "Tell me what to do." It was another part of boot camp. So I cooked some Filipino dishes.

People were interested to come, and there were 10 people altogether who came from our church. We set a gathering time at 4:00 for my American church family to come to my humble house-staff apartment next to Charleston Memorial Hospital.

After clarifying that my guests were coming and getting the final head count from the church, I drove back to get my lunch at the hospital. All the doctors and students received free meals. I saw Greenbrier walking in the cold Christmastime air. He was walking, as he didn't have a car. So I stopped to give him a ride.

I thought, "Good, I can witness to this hippie." Pulling alongside, I motioned for Greenbrier to ride with me. I was going to the cafeteria and presumed he was going there, too. Not one to mince words, I began asking if he knew where the Christian Medical Dental Society Group met in Charleston. Because remember, the doctor I met in Texas, Dr. Krafft, was the national president of that group. And he paid for my initiation to get my membership, so I was a member. Greenbrier said he was a member also, but they only had a group at West Virginia University in Morgantown. Now God witnessed to my soul. Here was a kindred spirit. Immediately I felt comfortable, presuming this young doctor was a Christian, too.

AMAZING

The Lord has promised good to me,
His word my hope secures;
He will my shield and portion be,
as long as life endures.
—from the hymn "Amazing Grace"

Greenbrier accepted my offer to ride back to the hospital for lunch after church. I praised God for my green Buick Apollo hatchback, which was a blessing I was happy to share. I was chatty, but Greenbrier was very quiet.

When I parked the car at the parking lot of the hospital, I said, "It's amazing. I don't know why, but it seems like I have known you for a long, long time." That's what I said. He didn't say anything to that, but that's what I remember saying. We ate together, and then I said, "Hey, if you have nothing to do this afternoon, I have these friends from our church who are coming to my house. You are also welcome to come."

Greenbrier did not say yes or no, but he hoarded all this food—milk, bananas, apples—that he could put in his pockets. In my mind I thought: "Oh, this man is hoarding all the food! Maybe because he has nothing in his student apartment." We got free food at the hospital. I stocked up, too, but I didn't get as much as Greenbrier because I was close to the hospital. I lived right across the parking lot. He was just a student, you know? So he came down and got all this food. He didn't say yes or no to my invitation, but sizing up the situation, I did not really expect he would come to my get-together.

At 4:00 p.m. all my guests came. By now I had adjusted to my adopted country. I was ready. In the Philippines everyone comes an hour late. However, I got dressed up, honoring the birth of Christ and my Christian guests. It was Christmastime, after all. And if you have a

party, you dress up. I had my long dress. I looked pretty, at least at that time. I was dressed up because they were coming. I was used to the Filipino way where people dress up. Here folks don't dress up as much; they are practical. I like it here. I don't have to dress up; however I enjoy doing so sometimes.

So anyway, Dr. Wallace was watching me prepare the food and the table. He said, "Araceli, do you have a boyfriend?"

I said, "No, I don't have a boyfriend."

Surprised, he asked, "Why not? You are pretty, you can sing."

"*Bola.*" I slipped into the Filipino language *Tagalog*, knowing that the compliment was not really deserved, as I could just sing a little bit with my guitar. I used that for the young people. But I did not believe my singing would win the heart of a boyfriend.

"You can cook," he continued, not realizing I was just learning. "Why don't you have a boyfriend?"

Now I became uncomfortable, retreating back near the refrigerator. Dr. Wallace was asking me the same questions that I had been asking God. He was offering the same debate points that I had been putting forth to God.

I was standing there by the refrigerator and Judith, a 45-year-old missionary to Brazil, joined the conversation. She was not yet married, and her mom, Miss Mary, was retired now. (Later on Judith did end up marrying.) Judith said, "You know my definition of an old maid? An old maid is the statue of the stupidity of man." That's what Judith said.

I was standing there praying, "God, I don't want to be a statue!" And then there was the doorbell. I thought maybe my neighbor wanted something from me. I had two or three neighbors on the fourth floor. They were all married with children. Maybe they needed something from me. So I opened the door, and it was Greenbrier.

I tell you, I was so embarrassed. It was Greenbrier! I

felt like I was very dressed up, and here comes a hippie, just as we were talking about a boyfriend! He had long blond hair with a beard. You know what he was wearing? He was wearing bell-bottom jeans with rick rack lace on the bottom of the pants and this leather jacket that had fringes.

We didn't have hippies in the Philippines. He looked really funny to me. I was so embarrassed, because I was with these conservative Christians, and here comes a hippie. I was actually very embarrassed.

Recovering my poise I said, "Dr. Almond, what a surprise. Thank you for accepting my invitation to come to dinner." Then I welcomed him to join my other guests. My, my.

I retreated back to the kitchen. I left him there with the others. A second surprise—Greenbrier fit right in. He talked to them and all was normal. I was really surprised at that. But I supposed an American could fit in with any American, especially because they were Christians. And they talked just like it was normal.

All the food tasted good. That was a small miracle! We laughed and chatted the time away. Then it was time to go, 6:00 p.m. There were evening church services. They had to go. Greenbrier said he would be going back to church, too. The Bible Center Church had night service twice a week, on Sundays and Wednesdays.

They asked me if I would join them.

"No, because tomorrow I have to work hard and I have to get up early," I replied, feeling a little sorry for myself. I tell you, I really worked hard. I don't want to go through that again, ever. I would rather just go home, forget it. But because I considered my residency as part of God's Boot Camp, I was determined. They could kill me with work or whatever they wanted to do to me, but I was not giving up.

I was not going home, I was not stopping, because I had already lost a residency. I was not going to lose this one.

No. I would just stick it out to the end.

After my guests left, I busied myself with cleaning up. Even though earlier I felt like I was having a blue Christmas, my spirit felt buoyed. My feet felt like dancing. My thoughts became more positive. I found myself declaring to God that I would not become a "statue to the stupidity of man"!

My lips hummed "Amazing Grace" until I sang verse three as a thank-you prayer:

> The Lord has promised good to me,
> His word my hope secures;
> He will my shield and portion be,
> as long as life endures.

BECOMING BEST FRIENDS

Greenbrier and I became really good friends over the winter. For his medical school rotations, he did a month of ER, a month of OB-GYN, and another month of radiology. He thought CAMC had more cases to learn from than WVU. He lived in student housing near Charleston Memorial Hospital. As a student, he lived in housing for students, not the staff building I lived in. This was the time in the early '70s of the first gas embargo. He did not yet own a car. My how he liked to walk. He jogged every day.

For Greenbrier's birthday in January, I recorded some of my favorite gospel songs, accompanying myself playing my guitar. He really appreciated it.

After the three months in Charleston, Greenbrier returned to Morgantown in February. He wrote me every day from Morgantown. For Valentine's Day, 1974, he wrote me a significant love letter. It was serious, but I was really not too sure then. I was happy to have his friendship, but I was not sure about marrying an American. I thought it was possible, but I really was not too sure. I knew I was happy to have a friend, and I knew I liked him a lot. I thought he was a funny guy. And we acted like we had known each other for a long time.

In addition to letters from Greenbrier, I got letters from the Philippines. My parents wrote me occasionally. I never told them I had problems, nor did I share about my dreams and my schemes. I did not want to worry them. Interestingly, one of their letters was marked "classified." I don't know why, there was nothing unusual inside anyway, just a normal letter.

Greenbrier could see the finish line for the marathon race that is medical school. First was the match for his residency in March. He matched with West Virginia University Charleston Division for his post-graduate training as a Behavioral Medicine and Psychiatry resident primarily at Charleston General Hospital of Charleston Area Medical Center.

By June Greenbrier and I decided to take the Federal Licensing Examination to secure our licenses to practice medicine. Both of us were busy. I remained constantly in the hospital with a very demanding pediatric residency. Greenbrier was selling his trailer in Morgantown and buying his first car, a blue Ford Mustang. Besides that, he was moving to Charleston. He spent time camping at his family farm they call "The Wilderness" in Hemlock, West Virginia. Thank God we both passed our exams.

We continued to grow together as good friends. I knew he liked me, but he didn't say anything to pressure me. I was just happy to have a friend. We shared common interests in medicine and in outdoor adventure. We worshiped together, making me so very happy to share a common Christian faith. I felt comfortable. I trusted him. He was a gentleman, a good guy.

We were becoming best friends, and in time would become much more.

FALLING IN LOVE

Greenbrier and I each read *I Loved a Girl: A Private Correspondence* by Walter Trobisch at the same time but before we knew each other. This book shaped our ideas of dating. God is so good. I bought my copy from a Christian bookstore in the Philippines. Actually, I read widely the books about dating and all the things that a Christian should do to honor God with relationships. This book touched my soul. Greenbrier was also reading that same book here in the United States. He was preparing for his future as a Godly husband. His soul was likewise touched by that book.

Walter Trobisch wrote of the Christian concept of not declaring love to a girl until you also declare that you want to marry her. Passion and promise to honor and protect come together. To speak of love only sets up the confusing emotions related to physical attraction.

After my five years of being pursued by an obsessive suitor, the Christian concepts sounded refreshing. When my suitor gave me three days to make a decision of marriage or not, I had no other life partner in mind. But in fact within five years I met Greenbrier.

God's timing was perfect. By the time I met Greenbrier, I stood independently as a physician. My mother and father were honored by that. Certainly my courting experience with that suitor made me choosy. Having strength of character, I could set criteria for a life partner. I determined he must be a Christian, with the same maturity as I or better, and highly educated like I. Understanding that physical attraction is part of a romantic relationship, I determined to select a handsome man who attracted me. While Greenbrier was very skinny and had long hair like a hippie, my mother's comment upon seeing his photo made him appealing. She said he looked like Jesus Christ.

So anyway, after being friends for a while, we were

now being identified as a couple. Greenbrier and I were invited together to Hinton, West Virginia, by a Filipino nurse. Her brother was a surgeon in Hinton. She invited us for the dedication of a backyard grotto during the River Festival over Labor Day weekend in early September 1974. So we went there. I was already in the second year of my pediatric residency. Greenbrier was a first-year resident in behavioral medicine and psychiatry.

We rode together in my car because he had car trouble. When his car was brand new, somebody put something in the gas tank, just to be nasty. So he could not use his Mustang. He lived in City Park Village across the hillside from Charleston General Hospital in low-income housing. Twice the police came to see him because a lady who rented below him complained there was a machine in his apartment that controlled her mind. So the police came. It turned out the sound she was hearing was from him exercising, using barbells that clicked on the floor when he put them down.

We went to Hinton to the festival. Greenbrier drove. We arrived there at 9:00 in the morning and our hosts were still sleeping, having celebrated the night before. So Greenbrier and I walked down to the Greenbrier River across the highway from the Cameras' home.

I can still see the scene in my mind:

In late summer the Greenbrier River is quite low. We find a large rock to sit on just off shore. Certainly God has made a beautiful day, with sunshine shimmering on the water. Kids are running along the bank, playing merrily. An older couple prepares to fish. We sit quietly and contently.

Greenbrier reminds me of the book *I Loved a Girl,* about the author's assertion that when love is talked about, then marriage must also be part of the conversation.

In a gentle way Greenbrier says he loves me. He asks me what I am going to do when I finish my residency, because I am now in my second year. He says for the first time that he loves me and wants to spend the rest of his life with me. For the first time he kisses me. We linger in the midst of the Greenbrier River, laughing and planning for what might be, "The Lord willing and the creek don't rise."

I AM DYING

One day during my residency in late 1974, I went home mad. I had been feeling great harassment at work. It felt like slave labor, so unfair. Greenbrier came to visit me daily. He had already proposed marriage. I was not too sure, as I thought Americans were very insincere and cruel. Greenbrier came that day and I told him in my anger, "I cannot marry you. You are one of them!" He left sad. He later told me he went to pray at the Almond's family farm, The Wilderness. I was very calm and said to myself, "That is it. I may never marry now." I was peaceful.

Within the next couple days, my voice changed. I got hoarse and could not talk nor sing well, though I didn't have a cold. I looked at and felt my neck; I thought I had a pea-size nodule there but was not sure. In the hospital corridor I asked a respected internist, Dr. Fisher, to feel my neck. He confirmed a tiny nodule.

Alarm bells went off. As a physician, I knew this could be serious. I ordered blood work on myself. All the results were normal as well as the thyroid tests. The radio nucleotide thyroid contrast with a dye was done to visualize my thyroid. No ultrasound or CT scan was available at that time at CAMC.

While I considered referral to premier diagnostic medical centers, I decided not to go to Mayo Clinic or other places where they had those machines in 1974. How fortunate, Dr. Lim, a Filipino physician practicing in Charleston, was the best head-and-neck surgeon in West Virginia. I consulted him. I was scheduled for neck surgery early 1975 at CAMC.

I did not tell my parents. I was afraid I would just make them worry, and the USA was more advanced and I had medical insurance. The best course of action was to undergo a delicate operation biopsying the nodule in my neck to firmly rule out cancer or to make a definitive diagnosis.

Indeed if the neck mass was a cancerous tumor and I was dying, I would go home and die in my parents' home.

A week after our argument, Greenbrier called me and began visiting me again. I kept telling him, "I am dying," when he visited me. This greatly puzzled him.

On Sunday three days before my surgery, Greenbrier and I were having lunch at the hospital cafeteria with another trainee, Dr. Hans Ruprecht from Switzerland, after church worship. I told them the rest of the medical story when Greenbrier asked why I was always saying, "I am dying." I showed them my radiological nuclear medicine scans, told them of the impending surgery, and explained my therapeutic options. I shocked Greenbrier.

He followed me after lunch, saying, "I love you! Why did you not tell me?"

"It was none of your business," I thought.

He still wanted to marry me even if I only lived a few months, he pleaded. What a sincere demonstration, I felt.

In my mind, I thought: "I will marry this man if it is only a cyst. But if it is cancer, I want to go home and die with my parents. I cannot let Greenbrier take care of a dying person."

A few days before surgery, I phoned my younger sister, a nurse in Dallas, and she flew in for my surgery. I wrote a personal will that all I had would be hers in case I did not wake up from surgery.

I woke up from anesthesia, and Greenbrier was what I first saw, all smiles, telling me it was only a tiny cyst. In my mind, I thought: "This is the man I am marrying!"

The surgery was in February 1975, and we got married Sept 13, 1975, at EvUnBreth Acres by Pastor Spradling, our pastor from Bible Center Church in Charleston. I may have said I was dying, but God had other plans for my life!

WEDDING BLESSINGS

Blessings from my parents were important for me, so I went back to the Philippine Islands after I completed my pediatric residency. How bittersweet this journey to the other side of the world for their approval. The Bible guided our Ganan Family. We knew the Scripture from Genesis 2:22-24:

> And the rib, which the Lord God had taken from man, made he a woman, and brought her unto the man. And Adam said, This is now bone of my bones, and flesh of my flesh: she shall be called Woman, because she was taken out of Man. Therefore shall a man leave his father and his mother, and shall cleave unto his wife: and they shall be one flesh.

My parents were letting me go, meaning I may never return "home." Reluctantly, permission was granted. I was ready to stay single if my father objected. My older sister Precy said, "How old are you? Go, get married!" I was then 31 years old. No one said anything more as I prepared for my U.S. wedding. I loved and honored my parents and was relieved that they gave their blessing. Unfortunately, my parents could not attend the wedding.

Life got quieter with Greenbrier around as our courtship progressed. Thank God for His peace that passes all understanding. We planned for our wedding, Sept 13, 1975, at EvUnBreth Acres, Buckhannon, WV. The date was chosen as I was done with my residency training at the end of June. I returned to the Philippines first for my parents' blessing, but also to prepare my bridal gown as well as gowns for my maids of honor. Greenbrier had limited vacation time as a second-year resident physician. Fortunately his rotation in September was outpatient, with some flexibility. Unfortunately, we could not go to the Philippines for a Filipino-style wedding. Besides difficult scheduling, we considered all the expense of such an affair. I knew he was a student and his American parents were not into high-style weddings. So we married in West Virginia, my new home.

PUTTING DOWN ROOTS IN BUCKHANNON

LIVING IN GOD'S GRACE

So we have lived in God's grace happily since our marriage on September 13, 1975. Believing the Bible way is the best way, Greenbrier and I have tried to live daily walking the straight and narrow.

Separating from my parents occurred when I went back to the Philippines before joining with Greenbrier. I sought the blessing from my parents, who could not attend our wedding. Receiving that blessing, we married at EvUnBreth Acres Church Conference Center in Buckhannon, "West, by God, Virginia."

God's grace certainly was with me in the healing of my voice, which got really hoarse after my surgery for about a month or more. I thought I would not have my normal voice back and would not be able to sing anymore. My singing was one of the very things I had dedicated to God when He gave me a guitar soon after I flew to California. Our CAMC pediatric cardiologist apparently was in the surgical room during the biopsy removal of my neck cyst. She mentioned the need to correct the placement of the endotracheal tube for the anesthesia. Perhaps the "voice box" sustained damage. But God healed.

Yet another time of divine intervention involved dental care. One of my molars cracked in half on its own while I was having lunch just after I returned from the Belize medical mission. On consult, a dentist in Dallas pulled the whole molar out. Earlier I had a filling put in it when I was in Philadelphia. Another molar cracked later in West Virginia when I ate some hard nuts. God granted skill to our dentist friend who is not only a great Gideon but forever our best man in our wedding. Dr. Darrell Milem, who is married to Marilyn Shissler, a best friend of Greenbrier's sister Ruthie, gave me a gold crown that still holds. PTL!

More times of grace—undeserved favor of God—came

at unexpected times. God and I shared daily without ceasing in prayer. My story remained unknown to my family. I never told my parents of having hard times or hardship in the United States. Even now, chronicles of my trouble is not the point of writing my memoir. I write so that God may be given glory. Many will be surprised I have gone through so much in my life. I even flew into the cuckoo's nest, making me feel insecure, but God brought me out.

As we fell in love, I told Greenbrier, "Maybe I'm crazy."

Greenbrier said, "You're not crazy! I know a crazy person when I see one!" Like a pattern of an Appalachian quilt which has one side looking very disorganized, I know in Heaven God has the other side of the quilt pattern of my life that is very beautiful.

So we grew thirsty for Living Water and for the Bread of Life food. We longed for a spiritual home. Our journey would be a bit circuitous, but God in His grace provided. Through Caroline and Herb Stotts's Sunday School Class at the First United Methodist Church, we found a wonderful fellowship of young Christian folks, many with small children. That was so good and right on time, too.

EARLY MARRIAGE

Our honeymoon extended into our first year of marriage. We lived in the Charleston Area Medical Center house-staff apartment building on the top floor in a two-bedroom corner apartment. I liked the extra windows. Greenbrier and I love plants, so we filled our windows with blooms. Because I love music, Greenbrier bought me a first-class Steinway piano. Down the street was Morris Harvey College where I began piano lessons. Soon our humble home was filled with music, proclaiming God's glory all our days.

Family has always been very important to Greenbrier. He wanted to return to Buckhannon to practice medicine and live close to his parents. He told me wonderful stories of growing up near Grandmother Mary and Grandfather Paul Flanagan. We prayed that God would give us children, but there was no pregnancy for nearly a year.

Planning our family nest like young lovebirds, we made weekend trips to search for a house. We didn't have money; we were just students. We were looking for a house because Greenbrier's residency in Charleston ended June 30, 1977. I told Greenbrier, after we had looked for a while, "Why don't we stay in a trailer for a while? It's cheaper." He had previously owned a trailer in Morgantown. Students stayed in it. It only cost him $3,000 and he sold it for $4,000. He made a profit. The trailer was within walking distance to the WVU School of Medicine. It had two bedrooms. I reminded him, "I have seen your trailer. It was nice. Maybe we can live in a trailer for a while."

But he said no, he wanted something better for us. I said, "I don't mind living in a trailer if that's what we can afford." His father could not give him any money. He was a doctor, but most of his services were free. Dr. Almond didn't get rich being a doctor. He was able to feed his family, but he didn't have more than enough to give away to anybody. So Greenbrier lived on his own, I knew that. In fact, I didn't even want him to give me anything he could not afford.

So we looked around in Buckhannon. There was a house for $30,000 near the Methodist church. But it didn't work out.

There was another house owned by one of Greenbrier's relatives, his first cousin, who was working at West Virginia Wesleyan College. It was near the Buckhannon City Library, but it did not work out either. But that got us looking around the college. Greenbrier was always thinking of children. He said if we lived near the beautiful campus, we could claim to have a 75-acre yard as a playground.

At last, we found a house. It was at 57 Meade Street just across from Wesleyan. He said it would be good for us, so we went to the bank, and the bank gave us money to buy it for $45,000. It was a frame house, a nice house. We moved there in September 1977 with our baby Maria, born February 3, 1977, in Charleston, West Virginia. The Hall sisters lived next door. Edith Hall was Greenbrier's fifth-grade teacher. Helen Hall taught him personalized typing in high school. And we loved our wonderful, spacious front yard.

GOD'S PROVISION

My brother Jun visited us in Buckhannon after we moved into our home at 57 Meade Street. By that time he was already in the Parliament in the Philippines. After I emigrated to the USA, Jun won election, serving as the youngest and I believe most effective parliamentarian in our history as a Republic. I remain proud of his service. Prior to our reunion he had been traveling the world. He went to Europe representing the Philippine Islands. After attending a United Nations General Assembly in New York City that fall, Jun came by to visit me, catching up on what his younger sister was up to. Ganans are always frank with each other. He observed, "Why do you keep this old rusty car?" referring to my five-year-old Buick. For some reason it had rusted all over. I don't know why. Winters are tough on cars in West Virginia. The engine was working. However, it was very, very rusty. "In America you don't keep a rusty car," my brother said. But we could not afford to trade cars, as we owned another family car. Greenbrier had bought a yellow Volkswagen Bug. We loved the size, style, and color. One time at about 2:00 a.m., I responded to an emergency call from St. Joseph's Hospital to assist a delivery and to receive the baby in fetal distress. There was snow on the ground and I was seven months pregnant with Roncevert. I almost slid into a telephone pole that early cold winter night.

Looking back to God's provision keeping us from harm, nevertheless, I believe the stress of life and work must have caused me to go into premature labor and delivery of Ronce one month early. Even then everything went well, though I was worried for the first day when Ronce would not suck milk from me. At 5 lbs 4 oz, and one month premature, he was too weak.

Greenbrier drove me in our yellow Bug on icy roads to deliver at UHC in Clarksburg where my doctor practiced.

Dr. Fe Lopez, a female Filipino OB/GYN doctor, attended the delivery. I was ready to deliver in the VW that Greenbrier drove cautiously as I hung on, not telling Greenbrier my fears of delivering in the car so he would not get nervous and wreck us.

What a trying time! I had experienced labor pains the night before and I was hoping they were just false labor pains, but I called my doctor in the early morning that I was coming to UHC. She would meet me there. I was rushed from the emergency room to the delivery room where I immediately delivered Ronce, who hung on to the delivery table paper. Greenbrier and I concluded from Ronce's tenacity that he would never give up in life. We rejoiced in his persistence even as an infant.

Oh what a joy to hear his cry! The baby was fed for two days on a preemie bottle and nipple, and he was placed in an incubator. Then two days later, he started to suck from my breast and got the real milk. PTL! How God blessed my son and daughter all these years to now—truly God kept His love, faithfulness and promise:

> Praise ye the Lord. Blessed is the man that feareth the Lord, that delighteth greatly in his commandments.
> His seed shall be mighty upon earth: the generation of the upright shall be blessed.
> Wealth and riches shall be in his house: and his righteousness endureth for ever.
> —Psalm 112:1-3

My doctor stated that since I had easy deliveries, I could have more babies, but Greenbrier and I stopped with our two children: Maria and Ronce. And what marvelous blessings from God they are.

GROWING PAINS

Greenbrier was looking for a more expansive building for the Total Life Clinic. We were outgrowing the house/office next to the City Hospital. Would we build an office or would we buy an old house and transform it? We were always on the lookout. Mainly I was busy with my children. I had two kids by now.

Greenbrier saw the Young house in 1980. There were problems with a hand-written will which limited the sale of the house to only heirs of the Young family. So, the scuttlebutt was that it could not be purchased. Beyond that, during the Jimmy Carter presidency, the bank interest was 18%. Nobody was buying houses. There were so many houses for sale up and down Meade Street, for example. Nobody was buying houses.

Greenbrier had a prompting from the Holy Spirit about the Young house. When he told me, I advised, "Greenbrier, we should pray about this."

"Let us look at it together so we can pray with our eyes open," Greenbrier said. "I want you to see this house."

I thought maybe it could be a clinic for him, being in town. So I went with him to this house. Mr. Patton Young lived in this 48 South Kanawha Street property alone. He welcomed us after Jane Reddecliff, realtor, made arrangements.

After inspecting all four floors and seeing the exceptional woodwork and stained glass windows, I knew it should not be a medical clinic. I told Greenbrier, "Greenbrier, you're not going to destroy this house by making it a medical clinic. It's too nice. It should belong to somebody who will take good care of it." I didn't realize that would be me.

"It should belong to somebody who will take good care of it." Our realtor Jane heard me say that, and she must have told Mr. Young about it. He was selling it for

$150,000. That was big money. We didn't have that kind of money.

Not really bargaining as Filipinos do so well, but in all honesty I told Mr. Young, "Mr. Young, we don't even have anything for a down payment. We have only lived in our house for two years. It's impossible for us to have that house. We don't have anything."

Bless his sweet heart, Mr. Young said, "I'll give it to you for $110,000." I thought that Mrs. Reddecliff told him what I said, that it should belong to someone who would take good care of the house. A fraternity wanted to buy the house, and a funeral home wanted to buy it, too. But Mr. Young didn't want to have his family home used like that. So when I said that, maybe it touched his heart to sell it to somebody who could make it into a home.

So he said, "I will let you have the house for $110,000. I will self-finance it at 8%." Self-finance at 8%! Now that was very attractive. I didn't mind living in town, because Manila is a big city. I was used to it. What happened next was simply miraculous!

I told Greenbrier and Jane Reddecliff, "I'm going to have this house. But God will have to make a way. In my eyes it is impossible, since we have had our frame house on Meade Street two years only." Jane suggested we put our house on the market as a way to secure a down payment. Now that seemed preposterous. Nobody was buying houses at that time. We would have to sell our house first, then we would have some money to put for the down payment and escrow, maybe $10,000. We didn't even have that. So anyway, we had to leave it up to God. If He wanted us in our little white frame house, so be it. If he wanted us in this magnificent brick mansion, so be it!

Three days before Greenbrier showed me the Young house, something else had happened. I was driving by the house in a car with my two toddlers and my niece and nephew who were living with us as exchange students. We housed them. We saw the "for sale" sign.

Mariette said, "Oh, there's a house for sale. I want to live on the third floor."

Bong said, "I want to live there, too."

And my three-year-old Maria said, "I want to live on the second floor."

Even two-year-old toddler Ronce chimed in, "I want to live on the second floor."

That was three days before. We were just joking, you know? It was impossible. We were just dreaming. So three days later, Greenbrier said, "I want you to see the house because I want to remodel it for a clinic." After walking through, I didn't want Greenbrier to destroy it, because the grandness of the place was meant to be a nice house, not a clinic.

Let me tell you, I am excited to give God the glory! How could I have been so presumptuous? I said, "The only thing we have to do first, Mr. Young, is to sell our house. If we sell our house, then we can buy your house." It was a good price, since he went down from $150,000 to $110,000, and it was an 8% self-finance. But we had the condition that we had to sell our house first.

We prayed: "God, if this is Your will for us, we will put up the present house for sale for one month. If nobody buys it, that's it. We will not move, we will stay here."

Five days later, a Friday, we were eating our meager dinner on our L.L. Bean folding picnic table in our dining room. That's what we had for our table, because we didn't have much of anything. We were just beginning our lives. Our living room was bare except for a retrieved sofa Greenbrier found. It was a throwaway sofa from a Marshall student. I just covered it with a bed sheet to make it decent. The only other furnishing we had there was a Steinway piano, because he had bought me a brand new piano. I like music, so he got me that. That was all our furniture.

So just as we sat down to eat supper, a man rang the

doorbell and asked if he could see the house. The real estate agent was not around, and our house was just what it was, but we obliged. He looked at all the rooms and our meager furniture. We quietly laughed at the thought of it at that time.

A miracle for sure, he said, "I like your house. I'll come back Monday." But he came back the next day and said, "I like your house, I want to buy it." We had bought it for $45,000 and were selling it for $60,000 in just over two years. He said, "I cannot pay you $60,000. I have to pay you $65,000." He apparently was a veteran. He mentioned a VA loan with point requirements. I don't know what he meant, but he had to borrow money from some sort of government loan program. He could not get the loan unless he got a house for $65,000!

Conceptualize how this can be. In a very difficult market we jack up our price $15,000 more than we paid. Now we have a buyer who wants to raise it $5,000 more. Indeed, the sale went through quickly and without a hitch. He bought the house for $65,000. It was a great miracle. And he did not even end up living in the house. We heard he got a divorce. The house was bought later by West Virginia Wesleyan College.

Amazing grace! We had *extra* money. Since family is important, we used it to fly to the Philippines. Greenbrier had never been to the Philippines, being a poor medical resident when we married in 1975. Our children, who we have always taught to be international, discovered the Philippines, too.

Greenbrier got to know me better than he ever had before. He visited my homeland and loved the Philippines. We had no trouble celebrating God's provision of $5,000.

We had to vacate 57 Meade Street as per the terms of our sale, but where would we live since the Young home had heirship issues to settle before we could purchase it? We were in trouble. Our home was sold, and we didn't know where to put our stuff.

Let me say Mr. Patton Young treated us as a true gentleman. The house sale was not completed yet. He told us to reach out our hands to him, and he shook them. "You come and live in my house until the sale is complete, free without paying rent. Put the utilities in your name. The house is as good as yours."

Furthermore, Mr. Young said, "I will sleep in a trailer." A trailer! He was letting us have the finest house in Buckhannon, saying, "You can stay in the house for free until everything is cleared."

We found out details limiting him from selling the house because there was a hand-written will that this house could never go out of the family. It had to always be within the family. So Greenbrier volunteered to contact his Buckhannon-Upshur classmate who was now an attorney.

"Charlie is sharp!" Greenbrier declared about Charlie Wilson, who helped us. He had us buy title insurance. He had all the known heirs sign that Patton Young could sell. Finally he set up a trust fund just in case there would ever be an unknown heir. Then we could buy our miracle house after living there free for the summer. Praise the Lord!

LOST AND FOUND

Surely our house is a gift from God! Truly, a miracle! A house gift from God!

Now recognized as part of the central Buckhannon residential historic district by the National Register of Historic Places, our home is described officially as "the Almond/Stuart/Young House located at 48 South Kanawha Street." The published description notes our home as "a three-story, imposing red brick finished residence with a symmetrical three-bay façade and a centered entrance suggestive of a central-passage interior plan." The description includes "the Palladian window centered on the second story of the façade and a large gable dormer penetrates the slope of the roof above. A nice feature is the open porch that extends across the façade, supported with square concrete pillars, trimmed with small medallions under the eaves, and enclosed within a solid brick railing. The once slate roof is now architectural shingles. The façade is brick reported to be five bricks thick. The foundation is stone. The style is Colonial Revival. The architect is D.C. Hughes. There is a detached garage which is special in its own right with a gasoline storage and hand pump."

In prayerful conversation with God, I reminded Him that if He wanted me to have this huge house, He had to provide someone to help me with the upkeep. We have mostly been fortunate with capable help, but one time a woman recommended to Greenbrier helped clean the house. I had the woman come to help, as I was busy with my patients. But I came home from the office to find that one of the mahogany chairs we ordered from the Philippines was broken. Perhaps in a clumsy moment, this lady may have used the chair and tumbled, but there was no report of her being hurt. My, my—lessons learned.

In our moving, I lost my medical school diploma and

had to ask my niece in the Philippines to go to Far Eastern University (FEU) to get me another copy, as I needed it for my application to St. Joseph Hospital to be admitting medical staff and to work in rotation in the ER with all the other doctors.

Fortunately, God has helped me many times when something has been lost. He responds to my praying petition with a reminder to check exactly where something lost can be found.

DEATH AND BIRTH OF A VISION

Verily, verily, I say unto you, Except a corn of wheat fall into the ground and die, it abideth alone: but if it die, it bringeth forth much fruit.

—John 12:24

I kept wondering about the death of our vision for the Total Life Clinic as we first conceptualized it in 1975. Different retreats of the Christian Medical and Dental Association talked of holistic medicine; of combining prayer and medicine; of medical missions to third world countries; of faith healing, etc. The variations on the theme were endless.

Each required planting a seed and nourishing its growth. What the messages lacked was the possibility that once planted, the seed may just die. My parents lost a baby sister Delia. Greenbrier's parents had a miscarriage, losing a baby early in a pregnancy.

Certainly we were two doctors joining together as husband and wife as well as partners in Christ and in medicine. Whatever he does, I do. Wherever he goes, I go. I am totally supportive of him. And here he was, forming the Total Life Clinic.

The Word of God is clear, but we were not mature enough in our faith in 1977 to understand what was happening to Total Life Clinic. That summer we faced many battles. The economy was very bad at the time. There was a mighty long coal miners' strike. Dad Almond advised us correctly that folks would just stop paying their doctor bills. They had to refinance truck and house loans, feed their families, and pay utilities, but doctor bills could wait.

What this meant to our young staff is that by winter 1978 we were out of money to pay salaries and had to lay off folks. Greenbrier had to tell employees that and they were upset with him. His mission was higher than the normal finances could afford.

How devastating to begin our clinic only to crash. Especially since our motto was Scripture from John 10:10: "The thief cometh not, but for to steal, and to kill, and to destroy: I am come that they might have life, and that they might have it more abundantly."

We felt horrible as physician and dentist leaders, but we could not do otherwise. Total Life Clinic's dentist Darrell Milem, Greenbrier and I were all active in the new Buckhannon Christian and Missionary Alliance Church along with many of the staff. We had overlapping relationships with growing friendships, employer-employee dynamics, and fellow Christians. They told the pastor about their feelings towards Greenbrier and complained about his leadership. So Pastor Bohman became a moderator for all of us, including Dr. Harold Almond. He was there. Actually I felt like crying, it was like my husband was being crucified. Greenbrier, he is a good and sincere guy. I know my husband. He is a very transparent type of person, one of the most transparent I've ever known. He is a really good guy, through and through.

Total Life Clinic died that day. The seed grew again, but that is another story.

From God's Boot Camp we learned a lesson about building a Christian group practice. We learned the meaning of John 10:10: "The thief cometh not, but for to steal, and to kill, and to destroy: I am come that they might have life, and that they might have it more abundantly."

Total Life Clinic when seen in context of Chapter 10 of John's Gospel embodied the biblical theme of sheep and the shepherd. The shepherd is accessible to the sheep. Strangers do not have a personal relationship with the flock, but the Good Shepherd does. Verse 10 draws the contrast between Jesus and false shepherds, the thieves who come to steal, kill and destroy.

Our God brought us through trials and tribulations, but not without some pain and suffering. We, the sheep, kept our access to God, the Shepherd. Our detractors were not folks in Buckhannon. Our detractor was the devil. Jesus remained true to His word in that our Boot Camp experience from the first year of medical and dental practice made us better healers for the next forty years of practicing the healing arts. We just kept practicing until we got it right.

A YEAR OF CHANGES

1978 was a year of challenges and changes. Our daughter celebrated her first birthday on February 3, and our son was born February 17. Dr. Darrell Milem, the dentist in our Total Life Clinic, rented one of our rooms in our modest house. We had a Filipino exchange student along with a nephew on the way to America to live with us. And we anticipated my parents' visit to see their grandchildren.

In early 1978 we had to shut down our Total Life Clinic due to difficult economic times. It was the death of a dream. Many of our staff were members alongside us at the Christian and Missionary Alliance church. They were hurt and upset about being laid off, though we had no choice in the matter. Our meeting as a church council did not resolve feelings of hurt.

A healthcare consultant had been hired to help us catch our balance with the financial balance of Total Life Clinic. He helped Greenbrier, who was feeling really bad about having to lay off employees for financial reasons, by pointing out that his professional and Christian work ethic had placed him in the 90th percentile of American psychiatrists in productivity.

We wrote grants. St. Joseph's Hospital opened a 26-bed psychiatric unit which Greenbrier and other recruited psychiatrists kept staffed. More mental health professionals joined our team on the Mental Health Unit.

Greenbrier and I grieved the loss of our initial dream but still trusted God.

BREAD OF LIFE

A slice of bread has two sides. Life has an up-side and a down-side. Jesus described Himself as the Bread of Life broken for us. I choose to believe everything about the Father, Jesus, and the Holy Spirit. The other side of that slice would be to doubt everything. Greenbrier and I lived out our faith while sorting out some sordid details of life.

How will God make us grow deeper so we are useful for His Kingdom? Greenbrier and I were still searching within organized churches. He had worshiped at the Morgantown Christian and Missionary Alliance when he was in medical school. He learned much in their Biblical studies and grew in that fellowship.

When we lived in Charleston, we worshiped at the Charleston Bible Center Church, which is basically an independent Baptist church. There too we learned a lot, particularly from the year-long study of Romans. Pastor Robert Spradling married us at the Evangelical United Brethren (EvUnBreth) Conference Center in Buckhannon.

We considered worshiping at the combined Evangelical United Brethren and Central Methodist Church upon our arrival in Buckhannon. God knew our hearts. We were open to His direction. We sought His wisdom. We joined the Christian Missionary and Alliance Church when they bought the old Buckhannon Evangelical United Brethren church.

After the church meeting with our former employees, Greenbrier and I ended up going back to the First United Methodist church where he grew up. His parents still worshiped there. We had each other, but nobody seemed to be friendly to me. Even until now, I sensed an interpersonal distance. Almost 40 years! My spirit felt dried up. Yes, I had seasons of showers of blessing but also seasons of dry spells. Overall, I was happy, because I was busy with my family, I was busy with my medicine, but I was lonely.

Seeking God's victory in the spring of 1984, I felt that something was wrong with this church. I went around the church like Joshua did when he went around Jericho seven times. I fasted from lunch every Wednesday for seven weeks, and on those days of fasting, at noontime I would pray. Even if it was raining or snowing, I would walk around the church. I would say, "I bind every force of evil there."

The Spirit is strong in me. My father taught us to seek God with all our heart, mind, spirit, and strength. Something was wrong, I could feel that something was wrong. The people were nice and friendly, but they seemed to be avoiding me, as if they were afraid of me.

Yet I see that God was in our decision to attend First United Methodist Church. We became part of the Stotts's Young Adult class and eventually developed lifelong friendships.

Greenbrier suggested we go for a spiritual renewal experience where the Holy Spirit was strong. The fall of that year we went to the Full Gospel Businessmen's meeting in Washington, D.C. Hallelujah! There a lady had a vision for me. What a shower of blessing! My heart swelled knowing God was not done with me yet.

SING WHEN THE SPIRIT SAYS SING

My, my. This seems like yesterday, but it was a long time ago. This was a Holy Spirit happening. In 1984 we were invited to the Full Gospel Businessmen's national meeting in Washington, D.C. We were curious. Greenbrier is United Methodist. That type of charismatic Holy Spirit expression is not something we have in our local church. They believe in the Holy Spirit, but they do not preach or teach about the charismatic gifts of the Holy Spirit.

So, we drove over to Washington, D.C. The convention began with spirited singing as the big auditorium filled up to capacity. The song leader created enthusiasm with music, and between songs he pointed to people in the audience and said, "God has something for you." Those designated would stand up, sometimes a couple, sometimes one person. I wondered about that. How come God talked to them and not to me? I was determined God had to talk to me. I already had that kind of desire. God talks to people, God had to talk to me, too. What if He had something to tell me?

The Full Gospel meeting ran for several days. The last day I prayed, "God, I really want You to talk to me. I don't know what Your message is for me, but I am going to hear from You. I am determined I am going to hear from You." So, I was praying about a message from God to me. Because all these people were getting messages, and I didn't get any. I was determined—I was going to sit in the front near the podium so the preacher would see me. After all, I'm Asian, and most of them were Caucasian, so I would stand out. I told Greenbrier about my desire, about my plan. I said, "We should go early today because we want to sit near the podium."

He was agreeable. Greenbrier goes along with me. We are a very compatible couple. So we went early. We were able to get a seat near the podium, three rows down from the front, near the podium, not directly in front, but a little to the left. Greenbrier was wearing a pinstripe suit, I was wearing a pink blouse and a skirt. So I was getting excited. I thought the praise and worship leader would see me. Nothing happened! He was leading the singing, and during the song he was pointing to people to give them a Word of Knowledge, as they call it.

I wondered, "How come God doesn't talk to me like He does to other people? He has many messages, but none for me." So I stretched my neck so the speaker could see me, but nothing happened. He was pointing to different people. At the end, the last people he spoke to were near us. He said, "The man in the pinstripe suit and the lady with the pink blouse." I looked at Greenbrier. Pinstripe suit and me in pink! That must be us! But he wasn't looking at us; he was looking beyond us about three seats past us. So the couple stood up and he said something to them. I don't know what the message was now. It didn't seem to speak to me anyway. It was sort of a generalized statement.

So I said, "Oh well, who am I anyway that God would have something for me?" That's what I thought: "I'm nobody even in God's eyes. Why should I expect Him to talk to me?" I didn't even listen to the preacher's sermon. I was thinking about why God rejected me. I kept looking in the back, eyeing the people, wondering why these people had messages from God but not me. And our clothes were the same as the couple who received the last word. Perhaps the praise and worship leader made a mistake. Maybe it was meant for me and Greenbrier; maybe he made a mistake. Because I really felt like in my heart God was supposed to tell me something.

After the benediction I stood up and followed Greenbrier out because we were dismissed. We had missed our chance. There was nothing more, the next day we were going home. As we were leaving, a young woman named Missy Cassell approached us. I didn't know her. She was maybe in her late twenties or early thirties. She said, "Excuse me. You might think I'm crazy, but I have something to tell you."

What was this? Both Greenbrier and I stopped. She said, "You know what? When that preacher was giving the Word of Knowledge to people, the room disappeared." She said she saw a vision. "The room disappeared and I saw babies. They were all naked and crying, the room full of babies. And they had chains and fetters on their feet, they were all crying out. And there came a woman into the room and loved them. As the woman touched each child, the chains were broken. And that woman was you!"

And I got excited! And Greenbrier said, "Yes! That is for her. She works with babies." Because at that time I was seeing children in Upshur County, practicing pediatric medicine. "She works with children." So I was excited. I was on cloud nine. I thought God forgot me. But God had something for me better yet, because if the preacher told me that, I probably wouldn't have believed it. But a stranger telling me directly about that, and she doesn't know me, I don't know her either—then I could believe it.

Pondering her Word of Knowledge in my heart, I left. I was on cloud nine. Then I told Greenbrier, "I think I have to go back because I have to get her name and address."

So we went back, and the woman said, "I'm glad you came back. I have more to tell you. After you touched the babies, the chains got broken and the babies grew," and she put her hand up high.

I tell you, even until now I am declaring God's praises: "I'm gonna sing when the Spirit says sing … and obey the Spirit of the Lord!"

My special Word of Knowledge remains wonderful. God has me helping the babies grow!

TURKEY IN THE STRAW

From my days as an intern at V. Luna General Hospital (Philippines Veterans Hospital) to my years of practice at the Louis A. Johnson Veterans Affairs Medical Center in West Virginia, I have enjoyed the doctor/patient relationship with those who fight to keep us free. "Freedom is not free" sums up my respectful feeling for veterans.

For me this a spiritual quest too, as I have heard many veterans quote John 15:13: "Greater love hath no man than this, that a man lay down his life for his friends."

You see, both Jesus and the soldier willingly lay down their lives. Jesus said God's love is like that of a mother bird who protects her young under her wings.

Thus I found in West Virginia many churches, many veterans and a rural environment—like the Philippines, a comfortable home. My husband, Greenbrier, sings these American folk songs to our children and now our grandchildren. He says Benjamin Franklin wanted the turkey and not the bald eagle to be the United States national bird.

Upon hearing the folk song "Turkey in the Straw," I quipped that this should be our national song, "by cracky!"

When Greenbrier and I married at EvUnBreth Acres, a church conference center at the edge of town, I was the only Filipino in Buckhannon. I was the very first person with Filipino origin in Buckhannon and was the only one for a long time. It was a tough row to hoe, as the local folk say, during those early years. I felt so alone and worried what would happen to my kids.

One day after I took my preschoolers to WVWC, I came to our kitchen and cried to God aloud, "Oh Lord, I can take the sufferings, but spare my kids." Something nudged me to go to Psalms, and I read Psalm 112. A year passed, I lived a life of agony and suffering and challenges, normal or not-so-normal that one goes through in life.

Then I praised the Lord when I realized that God in His timing kept His promise in Psalm 112:

112 Praise ye the Lord. Blessed is the man that feareth the Lord, that delighteth greatly in his commandments.
2 His seed shall be mighty upon earth: the generation of the upright shall be blessed.
3 Wealth and riches shall be in his house: and his righteousness endureth for ever.
4 Unto the upright there ariseth light in the darkness: he is gracious, and full of compassion, and righteous.
5 A good man sheweth favour, and lendeth: he will guide his affairs with discretion.
6 Surely he shall not be moved for ever: the righteous shall be in everlasting remembrance.
7 He shall not be afraid of evil tidings: his heart is fixed, trusting in the Lord.
8 His heart is established, he shall not be afraid, until he see his desire upon his enemies.
9 He hath dispersed, he hath given to the poor; his righteousness endureth for ever; his horn shall be exalted with honour.
10 The wicked shall see it, and be grieved; he shall gnash with his teeth, and melt away: the desire of the wicked shall perish.

Maria is only the second Harvard Medical School graduate educated from West Virginia for two centuries. She is making a contribution to medical literature by being published in psychiatric journals, has applied for a million-dollar grant to improve mental health services for five counties in Central Virginia, and is an active practitioner of psychiatric medicine. She follows in her father's footsteps, offering quality compassionate care to those in need.

Ronce graduated with high honors from Duke Law School and is now excelling, with blessings from above, in international law, particularly aviation law. He is a partner at The Wicks Group, PLLC. Bill Gates needed an international aviation attorney to pilot a bill through Congress and land it on the President's desk. The Bill and Melinda Gates Foundation has a vital interest in improving agriculture and feeding the world. There are agricultural programs in Ethiopia, Africa, that require air support, but legal regulation was constraining flying due to safety risk. Ronce was able to help negotiate policy changes, resulting in the U.S. Congress reversing their disapproval to approval, allowing the Gates Foundation to pursue its humanitarian project.

And God blessed me by providing good friends for me, particularly Linda Wellings and Judy Knorr.

Only God is Sovereign. Again, when I get discouraged about the world's situation, I beg for God's faithfulness and mercy and claim II Chronicles 7:14. I, bold as a person who loves America, remind us that we, as a people, are too proud and spoiled, and it is our downfall. We must humble ourselves before God and pray, seek His face. God promised to heal the land. He promised and will not lie. He keeps His words. Let us be bold to seek His face and obey, by cracky!

BELOVED

Beloved, I wish above all things that thou mayest prosper and be in health, even as thy soul prospereth.

—3 John 1:2

"God, I don't know why I don't have any friends in Buckhannon," I prayed. My father loved to sing "What a Friend We Have in Jesus." I said, "God, I need a flesh-and-blood friend. You are too far away there. I can talk to You, but where is my friend? I need a friend."

And then I remembered what I had read before: "You only need one or two friends, and that's all you need."

Always one to plead my case like my attorney father, I said, "Please give me a friend, one, even just one."

Greenbrier was here also, but I was not ready to tell him my deep need for a friend, because he is a psychiatrist. I didn't want him to think I was going nuts. Besides, as husband and wife, we are best friends. I thought he might misunderstand my longing.

What I am saying is hard to put into words, either English or Tagalog. But God understood my deep longing. He sent Linda Wellings. One day Linda was prompted to draw close to me. She is a smart woman, so perhaps she can explain the attraction and the friendship that developed.

We met in our First United Methodist Church Sunday School class taught by Caroline and Herb Stotts. Bud and Linda Wellings had moved to Buckhannon from the Washington, D.C., area in 1978. We both had younger children. Linda had two daughters and I had a son and daughter. We mutually felt strengthening our bond was important. Intentionally, once a week we met at Wendy's, across the street from my house, and ate and prayed. She said I made her laugh. She made me feel comfortable.

We were ambitious ladies believing that in God all

things are possible. Linda was an office worker at that time, a secretary at a small computer company by the Buckhannon River. The owner of the company mismanaged it, something happened, and it went bankrupt. So Linda and two other employees decided to invest by buying the company.

None of them had the required money, and they would have to get a loan. But we serve a rich God who owns a thousand cattle on a thousand hills, as the Bible says. So we prayed about it. That was before I went to Tulsa. God would bless my friend abundantly.

Here is what happened to her: they purchased the building, as they were able to borrow money from the bank, and they started their own company—MPL for Mark, Phil, and Linda. And then a flood came and flooded their building. So they moved out to the local strip mall. Then there was a fire and the building was burned. Disaster followed them. But then they found a rural setting at the edge of town on a bluff overlooking a peaceful field with the Brushy Fork stream flowing through it.

Linda felt God's leading. She said "Here am I!" She studied at night. She had married when she was just a young woman, and she didn't go to college. But now she was going to night school. She graduated from West Virginia Wesleyan. It was right for her. My best friend is a superwoman. With the wind at her back, she became a business owner, a college graduate, West Virginia Businesswoman of the Year, and president of the Chamber of Commerce. She is surprised by what happened.

Linda had vision and had our prayers supporting her. Even Linda cannot fathom it, because she could not have done it herself, on her own. She thinks it's because we prayed about it and God heard our prayers. God worked miracles in my life and He heard my prayers for my friend Linda. We serve a Mighty God.

As I told her, I am so thankful God grew our friendship.

ILL WIND

I believe that God has reasons for how my life will be lived. We are here on earth for a relatively short time but in Heaven for an eternity. Enrolling in God's Boot Camp and titling my memoir this way is my way of emphasizing the character-development purpose of life happenings.

I believe that when something bad happens in life to one person, something good is happening at the same time to another person. We are here on earth to be stewards of God's creation. A school of fish swimming in a Filipino bay can be caught for food to feed the village or can be caught by a Japanese fishing trawler to be sold abroad or to feed Japanese families. There are winners and losers.

Very seldom does something happen where nobody at all benefits. Likewise, an action or occurrence must be very bad (ill) indeed if it brings nothing good to anyone. Thus my father's adage to me: "It's an ill wind that blows nobody any good."

Anyway, I really think that government national security agents did follow me at some point in my life. Inquires made about me set up situations where rumors spread. And I have been judged without a chance to defend myself.

No wonder that I love James Bond movies. My mind operates like I am 007, subject of endless intrigue. How hard to be misunderstood! I have determined to live by faith with high ideals such as Truth, Love and Justice. But I have been suspected of base motives like Lies, Maliciousness and Injustice.

Some of my lessons learned are humorous to recall. In childhood when I was about 12 years old, my sisters and I slept together, sharing a common mattress. The youngest slept on one end of the row while the oldest slept at the other end. The sleeping one slept with an open mouth and the next older sister cried, "My, that breath smells like diarrhea!" And we all laughed.

Bad breath is called "dragon breath" in American slang. I am conscious of my breath now. Many Americans chew gum to cover dragon breath. But I do not like to be a goat chewing my cud all the time. While I avoid sardines if I can, I still love seafood.

Later, in the early '80s after I was already an American citizen, several strange things happened for which my inquiring mind could not find reasons. A nurse at St. Joseph's Hospital commented out of the blue, "What is the dead doing among the living?" Then on another occasion this same nurse said, "My life is an open book."

Yet another day as I walked from home to our Total Life Clinic, I picked up a magnet, like those placed on refrigerators, that read: "Don't mess with the U.S." I thought, "I am not messing with the U.S.—they are the ones messing with me."

Hmmmm!

What to make of these small, vague, seemingly unrelated happenings? Even as a 007 Secret Agent, I could not crack the case.

However, my faith in an all-knowing, all-powerful and all-present God grew in America. My life felt so abundant, with daily blessings as mother, wife and medical doctor. In my professional role, I felt thankful that some local mothers trusted me. I did my best for their children. I prayed a lot.

I come back to the theme of an "ill wind." Once in my busy, busy life, I did not brush my teeth and rinse my mouth, and I had eaten sardines before going to the clinic. A perceptive and honest young little patient said, "Your breath!" I realized I had dragon breath because of what I had eaten.

Another time in a Sunday School class taught by Dr. and Mrs. Herbert Stotts, my busy life caused me to miss mouth and dental care. Since I love canned sardines . . . there my dragon breath blew bad air again!!! I am very conscious of that now thanks to the promptings of my dear friends Linda Wellings and Judy Knorr. Judy told me to buy mints as a breath freshener. Greenbrier has never complained. Thank God he loves me just as I am, dragon breath or not. So far the wind blowing has favored my life.

UPROOTING TO TULSA IN OBEDIENCE

WHOM SHALL I SEND?

One snowy February day in 1986, Greenbrier was jogging as usual. He was about five miles from town on the Stony Run hill crest when in his prayers/meditation he felt an urgency to go to the City of Faith Medical and Research Center, part of Oral Roberts University (ORU) School of Medicine, because it was in trouble.

"Now is the time for us to go to the City of Faith in Tulsa," Greenbrier told me. "I believe they are in trouble." Every year the University medical school dean would call, saying Christian psychiatrists were as rare as hen's teeth. Would Greenbrier come? Every year Greenbrier would respond that he was meeting clinical needs here in West Virginia. Thanks but no thanks.

This time Greenbrier said his spirit sensed an urgency. He wanted to call the ORU Medical School to find out how things were coming along. Dean Dr. Larry Edwards said they still needed psychiatrists and pediatricians. There were six psychiatrists, but the City of Faith continued to expand. "We are not in trouble now," came the response.

Greenbrier told Dr. Edwards that he and I would begin to work on our license transfer from West Virginia to Oklahoma, which could take months. Greenbrier and I prayed for God's guidance as we remained interested in medical missions. I had already been on mission in the Philippines and in Belize. My heart was in missions. I began to sing the missionary-sending hymn:

> The voice of God is calling
> its summons in our day;
> Isaiah heard in Zion,
> and we now hear God say:
> "Whom shall I send to succor
> my people in their need?
> Whom shall I send to loosen

the bonds of shame and greed?"

From February to August we heard nothing more, but then one hot summer day I checked the mailbox and found a letter from the Oklahoma Board of Medicine. When Greenbrier and I opened it, we saw that his license had transferred but not mine. We were on the horns of a dilemma now. Greenbrier decided to call to get further advice from the dean of the medical school.

What we heard shocked us. Now the accreditation for the school was in question. Doctors in key specialties like psychiatry and pediatrics had left Tulsa. One lady psychiatrist had died from a major infection. Her husband, also a psychiatrist, was retiring, overwhelmed with grief. Two psychiatrists left at the end of the academic year in June. There were only four psychiatrists left. They felt the pressure of 24/7 practice.

Finally Greenbrier made up his mind and followed his spirit. The February snow run had been a summons: "Whom shall I send to succor my people in their need?"

We had to leave Father Harold, who was winding down his medical career. We thanked Mother Lois from here to eternity for her ongoing billing of our patients. These West Virginian mountaineers paid what they owed us for professional service, allowing us to pay off the construction costs to our addition to Father Harold's office at 27 South Kanawha Street. We did not want to burden the senior Dr. Almond.

More importantly for the foreign medical mission program, the young doctors we educated at ORU felt a call on their lives to practice their healing arts in faraway places like Africa and Asia. They did need us. They had heard the voice of God calling also!

GRASS GETS HURT

"Wapiganapo tembo nyasi huumia." (Swahili)
"When elephants fight the grass (reeds) gets hurt."

Swahili (Eastern and Central Africa) Proverb

Driven by a sense of mission to see the number of medical doctors on the mission field double by the year 2000, we moved to Tulsa, Oklahoma, at the end of 1986. The Oklahoma Medical Licensing Board would not give me my license. Period. They asked me to appear before the Board of Medicine in Oklahoma City. Greenbrier and I went before the Board of Medicine for them to tell me that they were not going to give me my license. They called me in just to look at me. Then they told me they were not giving me my license. They should not have asked me to appear before them. I tell you I wanted to cry, but what do you do? I could not practice medicine now. I was licensed for the United States, because I passed my test in West Virginia, and I was only seeking to transfer my license to Oklahoma. But the Board of Medicine people did not like Oral Roberts, that was why. They didn't like to give anybody who wanted to join Oral Roberts an Oklahoma license.

Greenbrier had received a license already. They delayed giving him his reciprocity license, too. When the American Psychiatric Association district branch of West Virginia psychiatrists elevated him to Distinguished Fellow, they could not deny it to him.

The Board of Medicine didn't have any case against me. They didn't have anybody suing me for anything. Eventually, they gave me my license, after I was already back in West Virginia. Too little, too late. I was not going back there. A medical missionary from Africa put all in perspective, quoting the Swahili proverb: "When the elephants fight the grass gets hurt." The concept of

180

combining prayer and medicine was fought by the elephants—Oral Roberts and his detractors. I got hurt, but I learned another lesson in God's Boot Camp.

I was granted an educational fellowship at Oral Roberts University at that time because I didn't have my license. So it didn't pay anything. Nevertheless, Greenbrier and I served as medical directors for the Adolescent Medicine Unit housed on one floor of the 30-story hospital tower. I also had an office in the pediatric department on a floor of the 60-floor clinic tower. We did research on a floor of the 20-story research tower. God got the glory.

The day Greenbrier arrived, Dean Dr. Larry Edwards, other department chairs, and my dear husband drove to Topeka, Kansas, to meet with leaders from the Menninger Clinic and the Colmery-O'Neil Veterans Affairs Medical Center. Providentially they found favor. The patient rooster and the facilities were opened up to our medical students. That literally gave us the patient load with the required complexity for ORU to stay open for two more years. Greenbrier received documents used in a successful review of their psychiatric residency, allowing him to write the ORU Psychiatric Residency Program. Praise the Lord.

Greenbrier appeared as a guest on Richard Roberts' live TV show about every two weeks. Richard Roberts, son of Oral Roberts, mentioned on TV that patients with eating disorders such as anorexia nervous and bulimia could receive care at the City of Faith. My, my. The phones lit up with Christian women all across America wanting to come. Greenbrier was put in charge of that 30-day program, with capacity for 30 patients at a time.

What a blessing to find that Dr. Krafft, the pediatrician doctor who mentored me in Dallas, Texas, was now working as the student health physician at Oral Roberts University. He was excited to see me.

God is good all the time. All the time God is good.

EVENING TIME OF LIFE

My mother returned to the United States of America quite ill. We had diagnosed her with gastrointestinal cancer five years before in West Virginia. The surgical removal of the stomach cancer was successful. She and my father chose to renew her strength in the Philippines. Now she came back to the States very emaciated and quite weak. We assumed it was a return of the cancer. Unfortunately, the additional work-up at the City of Faith provided evidence to support our clinical impression.

The best of medicine and the best of prayer joined together at Oral Roberts University, so we remained hopeful. Our motto adopted from President Roberts was "Expect a miracle!" Mother came expecting, but alas, she was terminal. We had her in our home receiving hospice care.

One summer morning as the hot sun rose over the Prayer Tower in the heart of the ORU campus, Mother told us of a nighttime visitor. Jesus came to the foot of her bed and beckoned to her to come with Him. She spoke of Jesus matter-of-factly without fear. We knew in the Bible God recorded 365 times the exhortation to "fear not."

Just as plain spoken as Mother, Greenbrier asked, "Mother, where do you want to be buried when you die?"

For some reason, my mother said, "West Virginia."

I said, "Mom, we are not there anymore. We are in Tulsa. Why do you want to be buried in West Virginia?"

We reminded her of burial plots in the Philippines already purchased as she and Father had prepared ahead. We pointed out that Bella lived in Texas, while Lily, Precy and Ned lived in California. No family lived in West Virginia except Greenbrier's parents.

Within the week, Maria Ganan did go to her Heavenly home. Nemesio Ganan, my father, took comfort in Jesus' words:

"And if I go and prepare a place for you, I will come again, and receive you unto myself; that where I am, there ye may be also." (John 14:3)

We respected Mother's wishes. Greenbrier called Buckhannon City Hall in West Virginia. Lo and behold, 16 plots in the old Heavner Cemetery had just opened up. He bought 8 for the Ganans and 8 for the Ganan-Almonds. The price was right. It was a small miracle.

At Mother's funeral we all gathered on the green grassy hillside, paying our respects to a wonderful mother. How special to sing the song of my new home:

> Oh, the West Virginia hills!
> How majestic and how grand,
> With their summits bathed in glory,
> Like our Prince Immanuel's Land!
> Is it any wonder then,
> That my heart with rapture thrills,
> As I stand once more with loved ones
> On those West Virginia hills?
>
> Oh, the hills, beautiful hills,
> How I love those West Virginia hills!
> If o'er sea o'er land I roam,
> Still I'll think of happy home,
> And my friends among the West Virginia hills.

HEDGE OF PROTECTION

The Mabee Center on the campus of Oral Roberts University was the grandest basketball coliseum in Oklahoma. Constantly Christian worship services were held there, with healing prayer offered. We doctors joked that we could not keep our hospital census up because our patients would ask for a pass to go to a healing service. Indeed, they would often get the miracle they expected. The next day on rounds they wanted discharged home, as they were no longer sick.

I attended a service at Oral Roberts University led by a lady, Evangelist Peterson. Her husband was a doctor. She was speaking in the auditorium. I was excited to go, to listen to her. I went alone. I was sitting in the back. The Charismatic people often receive Words of Knowledge. So I was listening to them, curious what she was saying to the people about whom she was given the Word of Knowledge.

Suddenly it seemed as though the time had flown by, and she indicated God directing her for a final Word of Knowledge. Evangelist Peterson pointed to me and wanted me to stand up. So I stood up.

"I have a word for you," she said. "There is a misunderstanding about you among your colleagues."

I started to cry. I felt God's presence right there. I felt God's presence in my life. So my emotions stirred, and I just cried. Because it was true. I felt misunderstood by my colleagues.

The Oklahoma Board of Medicine would not give me my license, whatever their reason. I started crying. The words of the prophet Isaiah came to mind. It is one of my favorite "fear nots":

> Fear thou not; for I am with thee: be not dismayed; for I am thy God: I will strengthen thee; yea, I will help thee; yea, I will uphold thee with the right

hand of my righteousness.

—Isaiah 41:10

Continuing, Evangelist Peterson noted, "There is a hedge around you. I see you in a field, and the grass is very tall." I have wondered about that until now. "There was a hedge around you." I thought maybe it was a hedge of protection as in the Bible. "There is mud on your feet, but it is not there now. There is a hedge around you," she said, "and I see you in a field. The grass is very tall." Her hands went up high.

Let me say, my faith increased. My mind reasoned, too: "My enemy cannot get in and I cannot get out, either," something like this. I didn't know what it meant exactly. But I felt protected. I felt embraced by a loving God.

That's all I can tell you; that's what she said. I still wonder about it, what it exactly meant. In good time it will come true. God will reveal it to me.

WHERE YOUR TREASURE IS

Helping young physicians become medical missionaries was our sole purpose in going to Oral Roberts University's City of Faith in 1986. And it was our "soul" purpose, too. Oral Roberts did not pay me anything because I was not licensed in Oklahoma. I was just volunteering. We stayed in an apartment for a while because we didn't have any money. One day Maria and Ronce got so excited. They began to yell for me to come and see the doors: "Look Mommy, hollow doors!" My, my. They knew we had solid wood doors in West Virginia but hollow doors in Oklahoma.

My younger sister Edna joined us so she could attend Bible School at Victory Church that met on the campus of Oral Roberts University. We sponsored her tuition, feeling she could have a role with the Odiongan Foursquare Bible College (OFBC) on our island of Tablas in the Philippines. We sponsored scholars in their third year of education at the OFBC. Students who made it that far would be motivated students, we reasoned.

After a year at ORU, we rented a larger house near the campus. When the Jenks School District sent information home about Maria going to Washington, D.C., with her class, we felt that this would make a better family educational excursion. We prepared for a vacation in July 1988. While away from our home we were burglarized twice. Oh, how we felt violated. Thank God we were away.

Tulsa felt dangerous to us after the break-ins. Besides that, the scholarship program for medical students was shut down by ORU. With $15,000 or more debt accumulated each year, our students felt they could not follow their dreams to the medical mission field. We prayed about what God would have us do.

So, we got broken into twice. They stole my mink coat that Greenbrier had bought for me secondhand when we lived in West Virginia. Somebody was selling a mink coat that had belonged to her grandmother, but she didn't need it and wasn't wearing it. So she sold it to Greenbrier for a few hundred dollars. Well, nobody wears mink coats in West Virginia. Actually, I liked it because it was warm, very warm. I didn't wear it much, but once when I wore it I got a picture, luckily. It was stolen along with the two computers of my children, an Atari game system, and the clothes of my son. He was outgrowing them anyway, and the computers were old. They were things that we didn't need anymore. They went through my jewelry, but we didn't have much to be stolen anyway. I'm not a jewelry person. I have a lot of fashion jewelry, not very expensive. But I do have a gold chain, maybe 18k gold, but it's thick, very thick gold. But they didn't get that. Maybe they thought it was fake, since it was with my fake things.

Then my mother died in August 1988 in our home from complications of her recurrent cancer. Her request to be buried in West Virginia directed our thinking back to our home among the hills.

During Mother's funeral, Greenbrier received a call from Dr. Erlinda DeLaPena, asking him to come to the Veterans Affairs Medical Center in Clarksburg, West Virginia, as chief of psychiatry.

Sensing God's leading, we said yes to returning to Buckhannon. Now two more events sealed the deal, not only as practical concerns but as answered prayers. A neurologist renting our house at 48 South Kanawha Street—with the solid wood doors—asked to break his lease so he could take a professional position in Colorado. Perfect timing for us! And as we contracted a mover to transport our belongings back to West Virginia, he told us the moving fee would be a little over $7,000, due on arrival. Well, Greenbrier initially told him he did not have that kind of money but could arrange for a loan in Buckhannon. Glory to God, when Greenbrier got our mail the final day in Oklahoma, there was a check from State Farm House Rental Insurance for $7,000 and change, reimbursing us for our stolen property with the exact amount owed the movers.

I am reminded of Jesus' command in Matthew 6:19-21:

> Lay not up for yourselves treasures upon earth, where moth and rust doth corrupt, and where thieves break through and steal:
> But lay up for yourselves treasures in heaven, where neither moth nor rust doth corrupt, and where thieves do not break through nor steal:
> For where your treasure is, there will your heart be also.

Immediately God showed Himself in control of our lives as we returned to West Virginia.

We had rented our 48 South Kanawha Street house to the Ryan Family during our first year away. He was the director of St. Joseph's Hospital. Then we rented to a recruited physician. About the time we were coming back, he was offered another job somewhere else. He had a one-year lease with us, but now he didn't know what to do, because he wanted to go.

What perfect timing by God. We were coming back. So I felt like, wow, how does that happen? So we came back and just took over our house. And we lived happily ever after.

COMING FULL CIRCLE

MY GOD IS REAL

When I first met Greenbrier, I felt like here was a hippie-looking guy I could witness to. For his birthday the first winter that I knew him, I recorded myself singing some gospel songs for his listening pleasure. Among those was "My God Is Real."

God's will be done! We married and began our family. This song came to me from the back roads of my memory when life was getting messy. We had moved back to West Virginia following my mother's death. I was in grief. I was at a crossroads in my medical career.

Pondering life, I took one day at a time. One morning I took my kids to school. Upon returning home the phone rang. It was the Chief of Staff at the Veterans Affairs Medical Center: "Dr. Ganan, when are you going to join us?" So, I felt like that was God telling me where to go. "I'll let your husband get your application." Greenbrier was working already there at the VA.

They went through the process, and that's when I told Greenbrier I would have trouble, because I thought the United States government was suspicious of me. That's what I think even now. I love America, but I don't know why I went through so much. I don't know whether it's real or not, but sometimes I even think maybe they hampered my board certificate. I don't know. I have no proof, because they said my records were burned. I also wrote the psychiatric unit where I was, the cuckoo's nest. I wanted to see my medical records. You know, they didn't even do a test on me for drugs, none that I could see. That is very unusual. Typically the first thing you would do in a case like that is test for drugs. I even thought perhaps I had been drugged.

I kept singing the old gospel song "My God Is Real," but I kept over-thinking. I even asked Greenbrier, "Am I crazy to think that way?" Because it seemed to fit. I was suspicious. Greenbrier rightfully said that I had a clean bill of health. First, the hospitalization was a clinical misjudgment. The work-up was not up to any measure of the standard of care. Even in his residency in Charleston, adverse drug reaction would have been his first clinical consideration. And getting clearance from the federal government to work as a physician proved there was no suspicion of investigation concerning my loyalty to my adopted American home. Furthermore, when I became a citizen I passed muster, too.

Yet, as a Child of King Jesus, I know there are attacks of the devil. I have heard sermons about oppression as an attack weapon. My gospel song addressed the fact that I am washed clean.

As I cleaned our gorgeous house God had blessed us with, I saw that the window sills had scars from burns, like someone used a lighter to burn the wood in the window sill. The burnt scar is still there at this writing.

I felt so helpless and was not sure what was happening and why. One time I was really crying. I was so unhappy. I felt people were harassing me. I didn't know what to do, because I didn't have any reason for it. I was lost. I could only complain to God. "Holy Spirit," I cried out, "You are the Comforter. Please come and comfort me." That's what I cried out. I was really crying, boo-hooing. Suddenly I was howling. I said, "What's that?" I stopped crying practically just to listen to myself howl. It was coming out of me. I was really loud, so I tried to lower down my voice because I didn't want others to hear my plaintive cry. We had exchange students living with us and I didn't want them to hear me cry loudly like that. I went through a lot but God's Presence sustained me. He remained so real in my life!

Thank God for His peace that is beyond understanding. Then I went on with the business of making a life for our family. "You are a mother, a wife, you have to cook and clean," I reasoned. However, that night lying beside my

193

husband who was sleeping already, I lay awake. I didn't sleep. I was thinking about what happened that morning, when I was howling. Then I prayed.

My obsessions returned. I thought: "What have I done, supposing I am right about my suspicions? What have I done in my life that they suspect me?" Then I thought about the White House incident, when my sister and I went there and tried to sleep in our car. The police there said we could only stay until 4:00 a.m. Yes of course, they had to protect the President, that's fine. But I thought about an FBI inquiry checking on me.

My mind returned to my faith in God.

Then doubts returned. When I came to America, I didn't have a birth certificate. During World War II all the birth certificates were destroyed. I was born at that time. Some clerk wrote my name but recorded the wrong year when I was applying to come to America. Now there is the dichotomy of two birth dates. My official papers list me as one year younger than I am. It is only one year, but still.

Also, I had claimed that I went to the United States Naval Base as a second-year medical student years ago in the Philippines. It was off the record. Now if they checked it out, they would not find it because it was not a formal thing, but a private thing. Some bureaucrat may claim that I was too proud of it. They may reason that I put it there when I came to America to brag falsely. Maybe they would check it out with the University, which would respond, "No, we don't have a record of that." Of course not, it was private. I forgot about those things, but the devil reminded me of my being proud about it.

You know what? God is so good. About 12 years ago something came in the mail, announcing that Dr. Richard A. Guthrie, diabetologist, was going to speak in Kentucky. My eyes grew big. I thought that he was the same doctor that had invited my girlfriend and classmate to the base, and she had asked me to go with her. This was the private externship I had been worried about. So I contacted the Kentucky State Medical Association. Wow! My mentor, Dr. Guthrie—it was him alright. So Greenbrier and I went to Kentucky. We had breakfast with him. I welcomed this opportunity to clear the air. What I rediscovered is that Dr. Guthrie is just a great American. He was reaching out to Filipinos. You know, he's just an ordinary man now. He's a doctor. But any inquiry, if ever one should come to Dr. Guthrie, would hear from him that I am innocent of malice. Furthermore, as we exchanged Christmas letters on years following, he could testify to my life as one who truly loves America.

Devil, leave me alone. My God is real! Faithful and true!

SALUTE!

From my days in an externship at the United States Sangley Point Naval Base in the Philippines, I have practiced the gesture of respect—the salute. Greenbrier also paid homage, or polite recognition, to his veteran patients at the Louis A. Johnson Veterans Affairs Medical Center in Clarksburg, West Virginia. We acknowledged a debt of gratitude to our fellow human beings who pledged to give all for our sake.

After my mother's death, we followed her request to be buried in West Virginia, and our transition home was easy. I came back to West Virginia where I had my medical license. The amazing thing is, Greenbrier had already been offered the chief of psychiatry position at the local VA even before the funeral was over. Almost immediately the chief of staff, Dr. Erlinda DeLaPena, began talking to Greenbrier. "Your wife is a doctor, too, and we need doctors. Can she work here?"

But I didn't fancy myself doctoring at the VA. It was all males, all the veterans! I didn't really want to work there. The children needed me at home during the months following our return to the West Virginia hills.

So one day I took the kids to school. I prayed, "God, I don't know what to do. I'm at a crossroads right now. I'm lost. I'm not holy enough for you to appear to me to tell me what to do." I thought: "Maybe I should open up a practice in Buckhannon, go back to that, as my patients are waiting for me. I am not a board-certified pediatrician, but I'm still fully trained and licensed as a general practitioner of medicine and surgery. I could still practice like other general practitioners such as Dr. Harold Almond, Dr. Chamberlain, Dr. Reed, and others. I could do that. It is just the certification that I don't have."

But out of the blue, Dr. DeLaPena called me from the VA, telling me to hurry up and get my application in to her.

She had raised three children while practicing at the VA and was now chief of staff. She was sure I could handle dual responsibilities. Her persistence paid off, and I began a wonderful medical practice serving veterans, including many who fought to free the Philippines from Japanese occupancy in World War II. I loved my veteran patients and they loved me.

While practicing medicine at the VA, I was the acting chief of the emergency room during a Joint Commission of Hospital Accreditation review. Thank goodness, God in His mercy allowed me to head our passing team. I was only two months there but very conscientious about my duties. I was scared to death because it was a nationwide thing. They came around for this critical examination of our ability to render quality service to our veterans. Glory be! We found favor, passing with flying colors.

Then I passed the advanced cardiac life support certification at West Virginia University School of Medicine. Let me emphasize that though Greenbrier considers me brilliant, I know my brain and diligence in study cannot alone explain how I passed. Clearly God had granted me favor. "Uncle Sam" elevated my pay grade a little bit for earning this certification, even though I was not board certified. (If I were board certified, I could have been paid more. But God still blessed me.)

The bulk of my career treating veterans was in primary care, general family medicine. I loved the vets and was so happy to serve them all. They deserve America's love and support, as they gave so much for all to enjoy what we enjoy now: life, liberty, and the pursuit of happiness.

I salute my patients and all veterans. And I salute God who provided miraculously for my medical career.

MIRACLE ON ICE

Three days before our flight to England during spring break of 1999, Greenbrier and I were driving to work at VA Medical Center in Clarksburg. Schools in Upshur County were given a snow day. Traffic was light and drivers were cautious, as the roads were not yet treated by the Department of Highways. How frosty cold! As usual, I was sipping a cup of coffee and eating a bowl of oat cereal with milk. The bowl was perched on the dashboard of our Jeep Cherokee. On Route 33-West approaching Buckhannon Mountain, we were following a big truck going downhill on a sweeping curve. Greenbrier cried, "I am losing control!" as we slid on black ice. Rapidly our Jeep slid into the left lane, turning 180 degrees.

I cried, "God help us!" and closed my eyes, preparing for impact. We hit the rough inside gravel, flipping backwards three times rapidly. *Kerplunck!* We landed upright. I opened my eyes, surveying the wreck. Our Jeep was on its wheels by the left hillside facing the road, as if ready to pull back onto the highway. The engine hummed.

Greenbrier was okay and I was okay. A lady named Mrs. Cutright was driving the car following us. She stopped and came over to see how we were. She was shaken up by what she had seen, declaring, "I have never seen anything like that!" She pointed to the rock outcropping on our left that we nearly crashed into. Then she pointed to the ravine ahead of us, of which we stopped short.

Like a smooth Strawberry Festival carnival ride, our Jeep flipped three times and landed right again without harming us. The front and back ends of the Jeep were smashed, but our cab was not harmed. The doors opened easily.

A West Virginia State Police Officer stopped next to check on us. The officer asked who was eating cereal. My bowl on the dashboard was upright and unbroken, its contents spilled over the front of the Jeep. My coffee cup was now empty. The unbroken cup had apparently hit my left knee, leaving a bruise. He drove us to St. Joseph's Hospital to have a precautionary checkup. No citation was given, but his opinion was that the Jeep was totaled.

Greenbrier told him that we had continued to live in Buckhannon though now working full time at the VA in Clarksburg. He quipped that statistically he figured we would have an accident driving that far for our careers. However, we liked living in Buckhannon, we explained.

The officer responded that he understood perfectly. He lived in Buckhannon but now was assigned to Glenville. He was driving to work when he stopped to check on our wreck. Likewise, he did not plan to move from Buckhannon. We all laughed.

"Seriously," he stated, "you experienced a miracle on ice." Hearing of my prayer for God to help us, he concurred that God did indeed help.

We called the VA from St. Joseph's Emergency Room, reporting that we could not work that day. Over the next day we recovered, being shaken up by what might have been.

Lo and behold, we kept our spring break flight to England three days later to join Maria, Ronce and my sister Bella for a whirlwind tour of England, Scotland, Ireland and Wales. As Greenbrier picked up the rental Volvo at Heathrow Airport, he joked that he would continue to drive on the wrong side of the road.

What a time. God be praised for our lives!

PEN PALS

A reader of this story of my life will learn of my lifelong desire for friendship. Fortunately my large family gave me many early playmates in siblings and cousins.

God put a desire in my heart for international friends—hands across the seas. Truly these bore fruit in my life whether my friend lived on Greece, Japan or America. As the Bible says:

> But the fruit of the Spirit is love, joy, peace, longsuffering, gentleness, goodness, faith, meekness, temperance: against such there is no law.
> —Galatians 5:22-23

I have had three pen pals in my lifetime. Two made big impressions. One was an American girl. She was born in December, and I am six months older with my June birthday.

Missionaries Jack and Aline Richie came from America to my island. They were married in the Philippines, actually. One Vacation Bible School they brought names of children in the United States who wanted to make friends with us. I chose Roanne from Texas. I was in third grade, and I chose her since she was my age. We wrote to each other. What joy as a young girl on a small island to have a pen pal from America. She sent me a picture of herself, but I didn't have a picture of myself to send. Our island was primitive. You know what she did? She sent me a Brownie camera in the mail. It came in the mail! But I didn't have film. You had to go to Manila, to the city, to get film. So I still couldn't send her a picture. But I was excited to have that Brownie.

For her selection my sister chose Priscilla because they had the same name. Priscilla Hester. I don't know what happened to her. Roanne and Priscilla knew each other. But they stopped communicating after so many years. So we wrote for maybe three or four years, until I was in high school and I got busy. I stopped writing. When I was coming to America, about 10 years later, I remembered my pen pal's name and her exact address. I memorized it and even remember it now. Roanne Warren lived on Easy Street in Crockett, Texas. I called her "Ronnie" because I didn't know how to pronounce her name. When I came to America I still thought it was "Ronnie." But Americans pronounce her name "Roanne."

My joy increased as I planned my move to America as a physician taking post-graduate education. I wrote her a letter telling her I was coming. I had not written in years. I sent my letter to the same address I had used previously. She never answered my letter, so I thought maybe she had gotten married and moved away. I never got an answer from her.

So that's it. Many years later, Greenbrier and I were married and were practicing medicine. San Diego was the site for the American Academy of Family Physicians annual meeting in 2001. Greenbrier went to one session and I went to another, based on our interests. In the group I went to, I saw a doctor there whose name tag indicated he was from Texas. So I spontaneously asked if he knew of Crockett, Texas.

"Well, I was born there!" he said.

"Do you happen to know a woman named Ronnie Warren?"

"You mean Roanne Warren?"

"Yeah, I think that's it." I had said "Ronnie," but it's "Roanne."

"We grew up together."

Can you imagine my joy? After so many years! I didn't know what God's plan was, but I was excited. We reconnected, and the next year Greenbrier and I flew to

Texas. We visited Roanne in Houston and then drove across the desert to "remember the Alamo" in San Antonio.

What a reunion! She told me she got the letter from me. Even though she had moved away, she still got the letter. But she never answered me because she was undergoing a divorce and was overwhelmed with her life. So she never answered me.

We joyfully caught up. Greenbrier and I stayed a night there. She has two sons, grown now. And she is a piano teacher.

Now we chat by phone. In fact, we are planning another face-to-face visit. She is a very strong Christian now. Her musical talent is used for the glory of God. Roanne plays the piano and organ in a church. What joy that she plans to spend time visiting us here in West Virginia.

The Spirit has borne fruit which continues.

TRAINING

Train up a child in the way he should go: and
when he is old, he will not depart from it.

—Proverbs 22:6

God trusted me, granting the responsibility to be a wife and
mother. I harbored doubt that I was good for Greenbrier. He
reassured me in those moments that God has a perfect plan
for our lives. The Heavenly Father brought us together and
we are one in His eyes.

And God trusted me with Maria and Roncevert, our
children. How special a mother's relationship is throughout
life became clear when we visited the Philippines when our
children were school age. They entered school as guest
students in the first grade under Mrs. May Ferrer. That was
a great experience for them. God let them glimpse what
being international was all about. Also, friendships began
which continue until today. Joy Faulan, Maria's friend and
classmate in the Philippines, is now a nurse in America.

While years passed, God revealed our family was
being properly trained. This occurred when we returned to
the Philippines after the children were adults. Maria wanted
to visit her old school. We walked across Odiongan for an
unannounced visit. As we picked out landmarks from
classrooms to the playground, suddenly a middle-aged lady
emerged from a classroom. She ran toward us yelling,
"Maria, is that you?" They greeted with a Filipino kiss and
then a West Virginia bear hug. May Ferrer was still
teaching elementary grades. As they laughed and cried with
glee, she paused. Rushing back to her classroom, she
returned with a plastic book of bright colors such as a red
apple for "A."

"Maria, you forgot your book. Here it is. I have been
using it to teach children to read all these years!" Precious
memories, how they linger.

A SWEET SONG: MY FRIEND JUDY

If we are all said to be different leaves of one tree, my friend Judy Knorr and I are blossoms of the same branch. We share a love of music, an appreciation of nature and a passion for Christ. Indeed, Judy and her husband Jim have become part of the soil that has nurtured the growth of my family and me.

I recall Judy teaching handbell to Maria and Ronce and other youth group members of First United Methodist Church. They rehearsed before their Sunday evening fellowship, often weeks at a time, learning handbell techniques and how to play together as a choir. The kids would watch in awe as Judy manipulated the handbells, spread across the table, from largest to smallest, from deep tones to high pitches. Through her graceful movements, ascending and descending, skipping and jumping, she created striking chords and melodic intonations, her white-gloved hands flying like fluttering doves.

Could they even dream to mimic her flowing motions?

Maria and Ronce followed Judy's lead, grasping their assigned bells and looking for their cue to ring out their individual tones. The discipline of practice—the example of Judy's steady work ethic—provided a roadmap for future success. Her natural spirit honed the kids' ancestral devotion to music. Their commitment to Judy, with her spirited directing, and each other, with each bell critical to the joint-production, provided early lessons in loyalty, self-control and cooperation.

Our children continued their musical education under Judy's husband Jim, who served as the choir director at Buckhannon-Upshur High School. Both Maria and Ronce participated in Chorale, the school's show choir and premier vocal group. As members of "The Buccaneers," Maria and Ronce traveled across the state and country to compete in show choir festivals and perform at public events.

Now Sunday afternoons were occupied with demanding practices at the high school. Jim even arranged for a professional choreographer to come down from Pittsburgh to teach the kids the arts of the stage. The pressures of live performance, the discipline of a skilled craft, and the teamwork required to produce a show were all important tests endured on the hard wood of the BUHS auditorium. And through Chorale, the world's stage seemed to open up for Maria and Ronce. We had taken the kids to Disney World in Orlando, Florida, to enjoy the globe's greatest theme park. Imagine Ronce's surprise when years later he would perform on stage at Disney as part of Jim's award-winning show choir. West Virginia's country roads do lead to amazing destinations!

And each Christmas, Jim arranged madrigal dinners for the community. The children wore period costumes and sang classic songs celebrating the season. The Chorale also performed a special Christmas-themed show at the annual dinners of local businesses and community organizations. Across the broad valley of Buckhannon, you could hear lovely ballads celebrating Christ's birth.

Jim's extraordinary talent and unending enthusiasm for his calling were an inspiration to Maria, Ronce and generations of Buckhannon's youth. He truly is the "Music Man" of Buckhannon. Unsurprisingly, one of Jim's favorite songs became one of my favorites—"My Home Among the Hills." My heart will be always in the West Virginia Hills.

As Jim developed the melodies of West Virginia through children's voices, Judy captured the images of its mountain rills through her camera. Her keen eye for waterfalls and moonlit meadows are reflected in her amazing photography. It's as if she could see both the natural and supernatural world bubbling from an Appalachian spring. This sense for nature was developed over a lifetime of farming, a tradition passed down from her parents on the family farm, a magnificent bluff rising above the Ohio River.

I was witness to one of her unique visions of God's creation. One summer day, Jim, Judy, Greenbrier and I decided to take a hike at our Promised Land Farm. We enjoyed each other's fellowship, laughing and singing along a ridge along the Middle Fork River. After several hours we descended into the deep 600-foot canyon, a trough etched from stony cliffs, our songs now accompanied by the harmony of the whitewater rapids. Near a natural cave formed under a cliff of sandstone, Judy became silent and then surprised the group with an outburst: "Do you see that tower? Look! An obelisk like the Washington Monument!" She turned to procure her binoculars, but when she returned to her original line of sight, the image had disappeared like a "rainbow in the mist." Perhaps she had sighted one of the tall oak trees or a rocky outcrop? Or was there a deeper meaning in her vision—our ephemeral ability to perceive God's perpetual presence?

I know that God's grace is certainly ever present in Judy's life. She is a constant reminder of the many opportunities to praise and worship Jesus, to sing of Heaven's promise, to study the Bible's blessed lessons and to save room for a spiritual retreat during a hurried life. Judy performs this all with grace and style. I especially love her encouragement to enjoy my time alone with the Master of my Soul. A quiet place is where I can sing a sweet song to our Triune God.

I am thankful to Judy and Jim for giving a musical voice to our "Home Among the Hills" in Buckhannon, for sharing a unique vision of nature's splendid gifts, and for providing me with a closer walk with our Savior.

HUA
Our Exceptional Daughter

Undoubtedly an acronym one will hear in boot camp is "HUA." When I reported to my summer medical externship at Sangley Point Naval Hospital during medical school, I learned the term.

HUA is one of the most widely used military acronyms. No one can agree on its spelling (HUA or HOOAH), origin, or even its meaning. It is commonly understood to mean "hear, understand, acknowledge."

Greenbrier and I knew that applied to our daughter Maria almost as soon as she was born on February 3, 1977. Maria had an uncanny knack of communicating with her eyes and her smile from day one. Since she was our first child, caring for her was a form of basic training for us both. She cooed for food or a diaper change just as if she were teaching us to pay attention to her. That is the "H" or "I hear you" part of the acronym.

Greenbrier often rose earlier than I to meditate on the hymns of the Christian faith. He would take baby Maria on his lap, letting her read the hymnal with him. Very quickly he was telling me that Maria understood the words and music. She mastered the "U" or "I understand you" part.

In fact, she had quite a vocabulary by two years of age. She read food labels and newspaper print, pronouncing words correctly. Musically Maria has a gift, too. We were pleased when she wanted violin lessons, so we got a junior size for her. Then she learned the piano, flute, and oboe, even achieving West Virginia State High School Symphony Orchestra status.

When we had a Brazilian foreign exchange student in our home the spring of Maria's junior year in high school, she traveled with us on our college tour. We visited Princeton, Yale and Harvard Universities, along with others. Our student's mother in Brazil requested the

Harvard visit. At the Harvard University tour, the admission staff said they only recruited valedictorians. Then they looked at "what else" the student might have to offer. I told Maria they were talking about her when they included on their interest list students with a South Pacific background, Appalachian heritage, and state orchestra placement playing a double reed instrument such as the oboe. We laughed at the prospect, but how pleasantly surprised we were years later when Harvard Medical School accepted her.

The "A" of HUA is "I acknowledge your statement." Maria grew into a young lady of grace. In grade school, her teacher, Susan Hansen, told us that Maria always knew the right answer, but she would carefully survey her class to see who might be raising his or her hand. With her eyes she would signal to Mrs. Hansen to call on the other classmate.

God gave Maria excellent friends in Buckhannon, including Cathy Leigh, Rebecca Webber, Kimberly Gilmore, Heidi Bradshaw, Megan Hefner, David Wiest, Josh Rollins, Jeff Poach, Carter Liotta, and Matt Menendez, among others. In high school Maria proposed that since we described our family as "international," she wanted to finish high school as an international. She asked our permission to apply to United World College for a two-year learning experience with 200 students selected as the best and brightest from 100 countries. We took her to American University in Washington, D.C., for her interview. Lo and behold, Maria earned a place.

HUA.

Later on she caught up with Cathy Leigh, her dear friend from Buckhannon, at Wellesley College in Massachusetts. This is the premier educator of women leaders. That Buckhannon, West Virginia, had two students of such caliber at one time at Wellesley is quite remarkable.

More so, how Maria matriculated is beyond measure. Literally, though we had grown accustomed to phenomenal feats of brain power, this was off the charts. Greenbrier drove her up to Wellesley College with our old Volvo jam-packed. At registration, Maria asked to test out of Chemistry for majors, Biology for Majors, and Calculus. The admission staff said, "No! This cannot be done."

Gung-ho, Maria reminded them to read their own admission manual. When they did, they found that the option was available, but they reminded Maria this had never been done. They advised against it.

Maria insisted that she be given a chance to try. Therefore, the tests were set up beginning that afternoon, followed by the next morning and the next afternoon. HUA! Maria passed all three tests, then completed the registration process, signing up for Organic Chemistry, an essential class on the path to medical school. By the end of her freshman year, she was honored as the best Chemistry student at Wellesley.

Surely another claimed definition for HUA as "refers to or means anything except no," also applies to Maria. She told us over the summer that while she aspired to be a medical doctor in the tradition of her grandfather and her parents, she was not going to take any more chemistry classes. She found English literature and writing more challenging, so she was declaring a new major.

With high morale, confidence, motivation and spirit, Maria sailed through college. She expressed her idealism after graduation by joining the Nobel Peace Prize winner Physicians for Human Rights. Her aim that year was to visit medical schools throughout America, advocating for the abolition of landmines. Innocent children in particular are killed and maimed by picking these up as toys.

HUA.

Amazing to behold, Harvard Medical School accepted Maria into their prestigious ranks the following year. However, they said they had strict criteria, including the rule that students take two chemistry classes before medical school. Maria, questioner of limits, discovered that they would accept any chemistry seminar Maria could concoct.

Greenbrier found Paul Richter, PhD, retired Wesleyan College Chemistry Professor, after worship service at the First United Methodist Church during fellowship time. Enthralled by the prospect of helping Maria be able to attend Harvard Medical School, Dr. Richter proposed a seminar on chemical analysis of the Buckhannon River water quality during the summer. Harvard Medical School said "yes!"

HUA.

MIGHTY UPON EARTH

Praise ye the Lord.
Blessed is the man that feareth the Lord, that
delighteth greatly in his commandments.

His seed shall be mighty upon earth: the
generation of the upright shall be blessed.

Wealth and riches shall be in his house: and his
righteousness endureth for ever.

Psalm 112:1-3

My son Roncevert exclaimed, "Mom, I have good luck.
The best circumstances happen to me."

Certainly as he approached graduation from high
school, his luck did not look good. Ronce did not know
what to do. He was kind of wishy-washy. He had not
applied to any school. His back-up plan was to go to West
Virginia Wesleyan College with a secondary backup—West
Virginia University. His dad and I did not believe in relying
on luck. We believed in God's blessings. We prayed for
Ronce's future and for wisdom to guide him.

Maria, his sister, told him, "You are as smart as I am.
You are just not applying yourself."

Good friends, including Ben Waldo, Jacob Hinkle,
Darian Cochran, Jon Green, Jay Liotta, Donnie Grubb,
Jared Feola, Randy Coffman, and Savinder Jaspal, tried to
help him out. Even their prodding could not motivate
Ronce.

So anyway, he hadn't applied to any schools. Then
during Spring Break, the Buckhannon-Upshur Senior
English Class Trip to London, England, provided Divine
Providence. No doubt about it!

While flying home from London, he sat by the dean of
Washington Jefferson College, a Presbyterian college in

Little Washington, Pennsylvania. The Dean was returning from Russia and learned Ronce had previously been on Christian Mission to Russia. After chatting a while, the dean asked him what school he was going to, since Ronce was a senior and soon to be graduating. Discovering that Ronce had yet to apply anywhere, he suggested, "Why don't you apply to my school? I am the dean, I can help you."

And Ronce found the match satisfactory. He really wanted to be away, yet not too far from his home in Buckhannon. So he applied, and he did very well there. In fact, he made an *A* in an upper-level History class for which the professor granted only one *A*.

Ronce outgrew the school, by his own reckoning. His History professor tried to persuade Ronce to stay, stating he could help him get into Yale Law School. Ronce certainly was grateful for the confidence-building experience, but he told me about Greek life that dominated the campus. He characterized it as "a lot of stupid things, Mom. I think it's stupid. I don't want to get involved in it."

His dad and he checked out George Washington University in Washington, D.C. Ronce had shown academic muscle as a freshman at W&J College, so he was accepted. Now his blessings continued. He graduated cum laude from George Washington University. Then Ronce applied to Duke University Law School, where he also graduated cum laude.

Believing in his ability, he returned to Washington, D.C., with a dream to pursue international business law. Blessings on Darian Cochran and his wife who let Ronce live in the basement of their house. We helped him with finances for a little while, since he didn't have a job but diligently looked.

Then the Wicks Group wanted him. They only considered top lawyers from top law schools. How happy we were as parents! Now they have made him a partner at the law firm. Indeed Ronce declares, "Mom, I have had good circumstances in my life." He is helping one country after another achieve international aviation law standards that keep flying safe. He has helped Trinidad and Tobago, Azerbaijan, India, Cabo Verde in Africa, Ethiopia, Panama, and the list grows. God has been good to Ronce.

On one flight he sat next to a woman, and they talked about India. He had been asked to be a moderator for a discussion panel, and the woman said he did a good job. "You are a natural, you could be on TV as a moderator."

God is faithful. That is a promise from the Almighty. Psalm 112 comforted me when I was crying, worried for my kids. To have a son "mighty upon earth" feels like such a blessing. At the time I did not know how God would do it, if it was a promise at all, but the verse comforted me anyway. I know now that God has a hand in all the blessings. Praise the Lord!

THY FAITHFULNESS EVERY NIGHT

To shew forth thy lovingkindness in the morning,
and thy faithfulness every night.

—Psalm 92:2

I want to be an outstanding soldier of the cross. I have tried
to be His child, anyway. I did not know about boot camps
until I worked with American vets at the Louis Johnson VA
Hospital in Clarksburg. God enrolled me in His Boot
Camp, I realize now.

I wanted to be wise like Solomon from the Bible. It was
a story I thought of a lot in grade school. I prayed to be
wise like King Solomon.

When my elder brother Nemesio encouraged me to
study medicine, I followed his leadership as is the custom
for Filipino families. More so, God had given me a glimpse
of Heaven with the healing prayer I offered to a sick and
dying duck when I was much younger.

In the name of Jesus I am grateful I followed my heart's
desire. I am grateful for leaps of faith making my journey
through life from the Philippines to America possible. Most
of all I am grateful that love never fails. When I became a
doctor, I desired to serve the best I could as a physician for
the vets. They gave their all for the country and I wanted to
help them medically. It was an honor and privilege to do so.

I could not see the process of my basic training. Since I
could only see through a glass darkly, as described in First
Corinthians 13, I could not foresee any downside to my
decision. Maybe I knew it would be intensive for a short
time, but I could not know how very difficult the training
program would be in God's Boot Camp. (This title came as
I told my life story. I hear how hard it is in military boot
camp. I thought, "I am in God's army.")

I did volunteer, trusting God's faithfulness. He would
equip me for future service, helping people become whole

214

in body, mind and spirit. I tried my very best with much prayer. How I love the veterans I served.

You know what happened? Many years ago I took my pediatric board examination. I had already taken the licensure test to practice medicine. I scored well on that test, even higher than Greenbrier, but for some reason I only got 10% on my pediatric boards. That's the area where I trained. I never did pass it, even after three attempts. It was always the same score. I felt bad about that. Not passing the boards has caused me a lot of anguish, even to the present. I felt so insecure, but it made me truly humbled. "Though You slay me, I will trust in You" was my prayer to God, like Job of the Bible.

Greenbrier and I reasoned that a doctor could guess and get more than 10% correct. I was just brave enough years later to write a letter inquiring about the results of my pediatric board examination. I wrote, "I thought I passed my test. Can you review the records?" Quite possibly there could have been an error in scoring. I received a letter back from them. My records were burned, destroyed after so many years, and review was not possible. I can't refute that. Only God knows the truth.

Even one of my attending physicians during my residency, Dr. Arthur Shawkey, also told me, "Dr. Ganan, I thought you passed your test." What could I say? I didn't pass it. I was feeling really, really bad. I thought I did, too. I was hurting when he said that, but I kept quiet.

Praise the Lord, I passed my federal medical licensing examination, and I worked for the VA. I loved my veterans. So maybe I was not meant to be a pediatrician; I was meant to be a family doctor. At least I passed my medical licensure exam. When I told my fellow VA doctors about not passing my specialty boards, they said, "Oh, it's just a piece of paper. That does not make you a better doctor than the others, or the best doctor. It's just a piece of paper. Don't think about it." But it still makes me feel bad.

In 2014, Dr. Lolong Firmalo, the current Governor of Romblon Province, Philippine Islands, asked if Greenbrier and I could help him with his hospital project in the Philippines. The Governor knows me. He was the best friend of my brother; we grew up together and were neighbors. He is now the Governor and a doctor, too. He improved the health care situation in the Philippines. He took the old provincial hospital and renovated it to make it more modern, as well as adding a new building. He asked me if Greenbrier and I could help.

Dr. Firmalo was in the wedding of my nephew last year. Still plagued by self-doubt, I didn't tell him I didn't pass my pediatric specialty board exam. But my heart has always been with the children in the Philippines. There are so many of them. I thought pediatrics was the best thing for me. I could help, but now I feel insecure about it. I could teach, but it's better if you have that certificate. But I don't have the certificate. I am now a retired physician at 74 years of age. I have balance problems and weakness.

But God is good in many, many ways. He saved me, so I told God, "Well, if You don't will it, maybe I'm not meant to be a pediatrician." I'm a doctor and that's it. I can see how God blessed and protected me, how faithful He is, and I'm grateful for it.

SERVANT LEADERSHIP

Nichols was a young American soldier who landed on Tablas Island in World War II. My parents and other citizens determined to hide him from the Japanese who occupied our country.

I do not know his full name, only his last name of Nichols. After the surrender of the Japanese, my father as mayor brought Nichols out from a secret location. The Japanese, however, captured him, paraded him around, and eventually killed him after torture even though the war was over. In Nichols Area, as we call it, outside the town of San Andres, the Filipinos honored him.

In 2014 I visited the area and inquired about the historical marker. Apparently they widened the street and bulldozed it. As a soldier for Christ in God's Army, I want to put the marker back there, even if I have to spend my own money to do so. I will place a big cross with his name near the spot he died. After all, he came from America to free us. An American hero indeed!

An American veterans' organization apparently came over some years ago to take his bones back to his family for burial with honor in a National Cemetery. He should have a marker in America but also one in the Philippines.

The present mayor of San Andres is my nephew. He is also a doctor. I can convince him that we should honor Nichols and our town with such a project. I need help with his birth date and his date of death. I don't know if there is any record in the town. You know record keeping in the Philippines is not very good. Perhaps the American Veterans of Foreign Wars may assist. When I Google "Nichols," there are so many Nichols.

The good news is, a month ago my sister said there were two farmers who were clearing up the grass near the cave where Nichols was hidden during the war. After so many years, one of the farmers wandered around and went into the cave. He found a medallion that likely belonged to Nichols. I believe God has His hand in this discovery. I told my sister, "Get hold of that medallion, pay for it, I don't care how much."

Now my sister has the medallion in her possession. I'm excited about that. The story behind this finding suggests God is not finished with His-story!

She put the medallion by my father's picture, because somehow there is a connection there. The American and the Filipino are intertwined once again. My personal belief is that this medallion belongs to Nichols's family. I don't know where the Nichols Family is, but my Spirit says they even could be from West Virginia. I know West Virginians who volunteered in World War II. Many Americans volunteered. I would not be surprised!

How exciting to have that possible connection from my birth home to my heart's home. Jesus said there is no greater love than for one to lay down his life for his friends. Thank you, Nichols! You will always be my hero!! Praise the Lord!!!

ANGELS CHARGE OVER THEE

For he shall give his angels charge over thee, to keep thee in all thy ways. They shall bear thee up in their hands, lest thou dash thy foot against a stone.

—Psalm 91:11,12

From my childhood I have believed God's Word. Mostly I have lived as a natural person with little of the supernatural to claim as happening to me. However, God has stepped in to keep me alive at times. Let me describe one such instance.

On the occasion of our hike across the top of Tablas Island, God saved my life. In May 2014 Greenbrier and I were hiking the Razor Back Mountain on the spine of our volcanic island, cresting at 1800 feet. Tablas Island is 30 miles long and 10 miles across. Greenbrier had wanted to hike the width since 1980. He likes to hike, as he is an Eagle Scout of the Boy Scouts of America. He had been dreaming of this big hike.

We support a Bible School in the Philippines. A student, Chris, and the chief librarian of the Ganan Memorial Library, Andrew Tiaga, who knew the mountain trail there agreed to lead us. Andrew is now the dean of the Bible school. Chris was at that time also working as a security guard, guarding the school at night, because he was poor. He is now a pastor on a smaller island. For 35 years we have supported the Romblon Campus of the Foursquare Bible College. Now we were sponsoring this student. He is part of my life now.

We were hiking up to the top of Razor Back Mountain in the middle of the island. Eons ago the hot lava rose from the floor of the deep Pacific Ocean. The final burst of molten rock made a giant curlicue like the top of a Dairy Queen soft-serve ice cream cone. We were hiking to the highest point. Early in the morning we were brought to the foot of the mountain at the end of the passable road where we could start hiking. We were happy, happy! I didn't wear my sneakers because they said we would have to cross the river eight times, as it criss-crosses. Rivers in the summer are usually low. So instead of sneakers, I wore my knock-off Crocs that I bought for $10. If they were to get wet, it was okay. As we walked, we saw such beautiful views, the Pacific Ocean on both sides. There were absolutely grand vistas in all directions, actually. It was my sister Edna, my younger sister next to me, with Greenbrier and me, and the two men from the Bible college, so there were five of us hiking.

Gradually the town of Odiongan faded into the distance to our backs as the town of Saint Maria appeared before us on the foggy Pacific coast. We were climbing above the clouds.

As we walked along, we saw cattle lining up in a military-style straight line just as we passed. Truly that is unusual. I wondered if they had ever seen so many people walking by. Perhaps they saw an angel or had a sense of spiritual wonder, given what was to soon happen.

Along the cow path we met a native with a gun who pointed out a seam of gold exposed in the hardened lava. He guarded his treasure. By custom he offered us a coconut cracked open so we could quench our thirst. Promising to keep secret the location of his riches beyond measure, we climbed higher and higher.

We began the final assent of the spiral swirl. Our former Filipino exchange student Maria Largueza planned to climb from her village to meet us in the air. Telecommunication companies built communication towers on the very top of the mountain peak. Now we carefully placed one foot in front of the other for the final 500 feet of climb up a trail only 6 inches wide. The ingenious Filipinos carried cement, water, metal pieces, and electronic equipment up the narrow trail to build the five towers on the highest point of this rocky perch. During our honeymoon in West Virginia, Greenbrier and I climbed Seneca Rocks, which is 900 feet tall. This peak is higher yet.

At Razor Back Mountain, it's very scary. The path is very narrow. You cannot walk two people side by side. You can only walk single file, carefully, like a cat. And there is nothing to hang on to, no rope. There is just grass. I said to myself, "If I fall here, that's the end of me." There was a little bit of cogongrass on the mountain which was sharp and cutting if clasped. In fact, I had a small cut from it on my hand.

I was thrilled with the vista of the blue Pacific to the horizon with the blue sky rising to Heaven above our Razor Back Mountain. We were praising God for His creation and for His protection:

> They shall bear thee up in their hands, lest thou dash thy foot against a stone....With long life will I satisfy him, and shew him my salvation.
> —Psalm 91: 12, 16

Here we were climbing the mountain. Greenbrier was up ahead, my sister Edna was next, maybe 4 feet behind him and 5 feet in front of me. The two Bible students were to my back. My sister cried out, "Be careful, there is a cliff here," as she stepped carefully through the muddy trail. We were now in the middle of the mountain ascent. There was a cliff to the right of 500 feet yet to ascend and there was 1,000 feet of cliff to the left. There was nothing there, no trees, no grass; you could see straight down below.

Now here is the miraculous part of my story. I don't know whether I passed out or I missed a step, slipping on a muddy patch of the trail. I don't know exactly because I felt like I was dreaming that I was rolling in pillows, then I woke up. According to Greenbrier, who had seen me fall, I had fallen headfirst in a forward roll over the edge, potentially tumbling 1500 feet down to a very traumatic end. I landed about 12 feet down below the trail.

The Bible students could not climb down to my small perch on the very edge of the cliff. They would surely tumble. But once I gathered myself and was fully awake, I climbed back up, making my way to my left where there was a foothold. Finally, they reached out for me to pull me up the final 5 feet. Praise the Lord, everything was alright except my watch which had fallen off when I fell and was hanging on the edge of the cliff. I didn't even have a scratch or a bruise, nothing. Not even my clothes were ruined. My sandals were there, my glasses were fine and still in place. I really should have been in a panic, but I was just peaceful.

I never thought of it at the time as a miracle. It was only after the fact that I realized, wow, I never had even a scratch. How can that be?

So anyway, we walked on, then we saw a banana that was fully ripe. It was a wild banana. Andrew pushed the limb down so we could get the banana. According to Greenbrier, it was one of the sweetest bananas he had ever tasted. After that we went on to the communication tower and met our friend Maria Largueza and the others we were supposed to meet there.

After a while we went down another route to get back to where we came from so we could go home. Then we passed along another spine of the mountain, and the grass was tall. I was afraid there were snakes. I'm scared of snakes. So I had a stick which I slapped in front of me to drive away any snakes before I passed by. We went on to a church down below that belonged to one of the students. He wanted to pass that way because apparently he wanted to introduce us to his family. All the family—the father, the mother, the sister and a baby—were there. They gave us water to drink, the water that belonged to the baby, but they were gracious enough to give it to us.

Then it was dark already, as the sun was down. It was 6:30 p.m. We couldn't see a thing. We didn't have a flashlight; we never expected to be out there in the dark. So I hung on to Andrew, one of the Bible students. I hung on to him because it was very slippery going downhill now. It had rained a few days before, so the road was slippery. I was scared that I would fall and slip. I didn't want to do that after falling from the cliff.

We used the cellphone lights to light our pathway. We went to a church that owned motorcycles. Andrew asked the pastor there, whom he knew, if we could borrow three motorcycles to take us to the main road where we could catch another ride. The pastor said yes, we could borrow their three motorcycles.

Greenbrier wants nothing to do with motorcycles. He thinks if he has an accident, that's the end of him. And he certainly didn't want any major accident on the island. But I was so tired, I was worn out, so I rode one of the cycles. My sister rode on another one, and Chris on the other. We were just too worn out to do anything, I didn't care anymore. The driver of my motorcycle was the son of the pastor, so he knew the area well. He must have used that motorcycle himself and was glad to give us a ride, even in the dark of early evening.

My goodness, he was driving fast. There was one of the eight river crossings ahead. The riverbank was a cliff ahead of us. I just closed my eyes, thinking that was the end of me. This motorcycle would jump into the river and that would be my end. I was waiting for my demise. I just closed my eyes. But then suddenly he turned left, down, then crossed the river. The river was shallow anyway, maybe ankle-deep. We reached the other side of the river, and I thought, "Oh, now he will let us off." I was ready to get off, because we were climbing again on the cliff. But he didn't even ask me to get off the motorcycle. He just changed gears, and off we went again. I just closed my eyes.

I tell you, I was so scared. In my life, I never want to do it again! Greenbrier would rather walk the one mile to the main road than to ride the motorcycle. And he did, along with Andrew.

We made it back at last. We were so hungry we didn't know what to do. All the restaurants on the island were closed, except one, so we went to eat. We treated the Bible students to a meal, then we went home singing and praising God:

> He that dwelleth in the secret place of the most High shall abide under the shadow of the Almighty. I will say of the LORD, He is my refuge and my fortress: my God; in him will I trust.
>
> —Psalm 91:1, 2

MUSINGS

"DO YOU LOVE ME?"

We choose sides when playing games as children, but a lesson learned in life is that God does not favor one side or another in human terms. Whether one is a Filipino Catholic or a nominal Catholic or not a Catholic does not make one less of a child of God.

While I have discovered by coming to the USA that Filipino Catholics are different from American Catholics. I have realized a greater discovery about God and The Holy Trinity that is Love! When Christ comes back He will not ask, "Are you Methodist? Are you Baptist? Are you this, are you that?" He will only say, "Do you know me? Do you love me?" That's the main thing. I think denomination does not matter to Him.

Worshiping God comes when we open our hearts to God as we understand Him. But for me, of course, after growing up in a Foursquare Gospel Church, I'm grateful for their worship services. Greenbrier and I help the Romblon Campus of the Foursquare Bible College. Here in West Virginia we both worship at Greenbrier's home church, First United Methodist Church, where his parents brought him at two years of age. The United Methodist Churches in our town, along with West Virginia Wesleyan College, provide a vital community of faith. Here we love God and feel His love in turn.

I became an American citizen in November 1977, after Maria was born and I was pregnant with Ronce. Part of my love for America and its people came from knowing the American Christians who came as missionaries bringing the Good News of God's love to Tablas Island. Now, I believe that God has reasons for my life experiences. "His Eye Is on the Sparrow," a favorite song of mine, tells of God's love for even me the least of His children. He has plans that I know not, but I have told God in prayer that I will obey. So be it with His help. God is with me, who can be against me? God's purpose will prevail in my life. More will be revealed and I anticipate it. To God be the Glory!

Yes, as Jesus said, "Anyone who follows me will be persecuted," so I anticipate hardship. "No servant is above his master." I realize I actually enrolled in God's Boot Camp, not knowing His wonderful plan for my life.

COME FORTH AS GOLD

When I accepted Jesus in my heart by going forward to the altar in my church in the Philippines, I knew God's Way was the best way to live a full life. Even though life has had struggles, I have remained true to my vow made when I was 14 years old.

> But he knoweth the way that I take: when he hath tried me, I shall come forth as gold.
>
> Job 23:10

Certainly, like any soldier in boot camp, I have had my testings and trials. I have asked "why?" many times. Christian books have served as road maps for me, including those by Oswald Chambers, who said, "There will come one day a personal and direct touch from God when every tear and perplexity, every oppression and distress, every suffering and pain, and wrong and injustice will have a complete and ample and overwhelming explanation."

As I have told you, my reader, I have had words from God, such as at the Full Gospel Businessmen's Meeting in 1984 and later from Australian evangelist Shane Cunningham in 2014 in the Philippines.

After some time I would think about these things, what they meant in my life. Pondering and asking "why?" has led me deeper in my understanding of God's way.

My husband, Greenbrier, has had spiritual moments, too. Our life was forever changed by his jogging one snowy day in February 1986. The still small voice of God spoke to him about moving to Tulsa, Oklahoma, to teach Christian medical students at Oral Roberts University School of Medicine, who, in turn, felt God's calling to the medical mission field.

Our response served us well as a "come forth as gold" life event. As in an army, we were not on the front lines of battle but were support to soldiers going where "God's voice is small," as Oral Roberts preached. I'm just Greenbrier's wife; however, I was happy to go! So we told our patients we were leaving for Tulsa and things worked out for him.

We were staying in an apartment for a while, all of our stuff packed in storage. Oral Roberts University paid our moving costs to Oklahoma. We had accumulated a lot of stuff. One lesson learned is that we did not need most of it. For two years some boxes were never unpacked.

My emphasis in my memoir is to declare that God provides all we need. We certainly have options to have "stuff," but much of that needs to be given away. Our custom is to pack "Balikbayan boxes" for the Philippines with items we do not need. Some poor families will count what we send as manna from Heaven.

God provided for our needs in Tulsa even without my salary, since I volunteered without pay. When we returned to West Virginia, my medical license was good. The children were older. God provided work for us both at the Veterans Affairs Medical Center in Clarksburg.

We count God's provision of the rental insurance money down to the very dollar owed to the moving van company the very day we were moving home, as a big sign of His Love. We got broken into twice in Tulsa. They stole various items, including my mink coat. But one thing they did not get was the real gold chain I have. It's thick. It was hanging there, but they didn't take it. Maybe they thought it was fake. And one of my mother's earrings, an antique diamond, was there on the floor. I'm glad they didn't take it. Literally, I came forth with what was valuable as gold!

YE SHALL HAVE DOUBLE

> For your shame ye shall have double; and for confusion they shall rejoice in their portion: therefore in their land they shall possess the double: everlasting joy shall be unto them.
>
> —Isaiah 61:7

We have identified ourselves as the "Almond Joys" from day one of our marriage. And when Maria and Ronce were born, we handed out Almond Joy candy bars instead of cigars. How perfect that in my year of Jubilee God gave me Isaiah 61 as Scripture for my meditation.

Perfect because, as I told my husband, I lost my psychiatric residency years ago. But when my daughter Maria and her husband Justin moved to Michigan and started their family with Aliza (Hebrew for "the trees clapping their leaves with joy") and Emilia Sylvie ("eager trees"), I realized God has given me a double portion. For Greenbrier is a psychiatrist and Maria is a psychiatrist.

Wow! I have doubled my portion. I have two psychiatrists, even though I lost my own psychiatry residency. But God blessed me with two psychiatrists in my family. Then my daughter actually became the clinical director of the psychiatry oncology department of the University of Michigan. I pondered that. I thought, "This is the place that called me out of the blue about going there for an internal medicine residency." But at the time I didn't even know anybody there. God's leading was to West Virginia.

Scripture provides the foundation for my belief. I dare not trust my own feelings, though I pay attention to them. Now in 2016 I sit under the preaching of Pastor Steve Meadows. He is the best pastor I think I have ever had. I hear the Word of God through Pastor Meadows's preaching. It seems like he knows about me. One time I told Greenbrier, "He knows about me. He was preaching about me."

When I told Greenbrier, he said, "Yes of course, any pastor will preach about Jesus Christ, and what He went through. It's what you are going through. It looks like it's you but it's for everybody." Scripture remains the final arbiter of my life experience. In reading the Bible, for instance Isaiah 61, I find great joy.

Here is yet another example of the Bible guiding my life. Before I went to Central America for medical mission with *Amigos Internationales*, Dr. Krafft took me to a church, to the pastor's study room. I sat there at the big desk. The pastor said, "God is Spirit, and we should worship God in Spirit and in Truth." I know those verses from John 4:24. And then he said, "And the truth shall set you free." So I wondered about it. I didn't get the whole meaning for my life at that time. But I recall that now. As I adventured in Belize, prayerfully God's truth came to me. Much happened in Central America for which I could rejoice even in my confusion.

Hard times in West Virginia at times have been my lot and portion. I've asked, "Why, why, why? Why is everything bad following me?" I've felt oppressed.

But I remained determined. I was not going to stop my residency. They could kill me, they could overwork me. So what? I was not going to stop and go home. I was determined that I was going to get my medical program finished, because I had already lost a program. I finished everything they wanted me to do. I stuck around.

> For your shame ye shall have double; and for confusion they shall rejoice in their portion: therefore in their land they shall possess the double: everlasting joy shall be unto them.
> —Isaiah 61:7

PLEASANT DREAM

In a dream that I distinctly remember, I see myself dancing with an American man, and he tells me he loves me very much. Indeed, I am enjoying his attention and agility as we whirl in dance around the room. My father raised us conservatively, not allowing dance. So in my dream, at first I do not want to enter the dance hall.

My anxiety centers around meeting someone with whom I seem to have had a previous relationship. Immediately after that moment of hesitation, I am dancing with the person I tried to avoid.

After awhile, I look at my watch and say, "It is three o'clock now and I must go. Greenbrier is waiting for me." Then suddenly I am in another room where a woman asks me if I want a piece of the carpet that I danced on. Or would I like the decorations on the wall?

"No, this is all I need," I say, holding an egg on a paper plate that must be left over from the party.

Suddenly I am outside on the front porch of the building with Greenbrier. We are facing east and the huge morning sun is shining brightly. The portico columns are impressive. It is like what I see in Washington, D.C., at the U.S. Capitol or Supreme Court building. There are just the columns in my dream, no roof, just rows of columns.

Then I woke up at 3:00, which is the time I had said in my dream! I pondered on the dream. How strange to remember, even now, every bit of it. My dreams are usually shallow and forgotten, but this one stands out. I wonder, what does the dream mean?

"Where there is no vision, the people perish: but he that keepeth the law, happy is he." This is what Solomon recorded in Proverbs 29:18. As a child I prayed for wisdom. While I have an idea that perhaps my dream is a vision given by God, telling me my life past to future, I do not want to think too grandiose. My mother taught me to be careful. My father taught me to be prudent. Only God knows why He gave me this dream. And He holds me in the palm of His hand. To God be honor and glory, forever!

WITH THE HEART

A delight of being a mother and a *lola* (grandmother) is reading stories to the grandchildren. A book discovered and rediscovered is *The Little Prince*. If Saint-Exupéry is to be believed, *The Little Prince* is a children's book written for grown-ups. There are different levels of interpretation for readers of all ages to ponder and enjoy.

As I write my memoir for the grandchildren, I am reminded:

> One sees clearly only with the heart. Anything essential is invisible to the eye.
>
> —*The Little Prince*

After my short stint in the cuckoo's nest, which was a nightmare, I went on and tried to take things in stride. God's grace was with me. What else can I say? My parents were not here to help me; nobody else was here to help me. I just went on with my life. But I developed an attitude of gratitude.

I had negative feelings from feeling harassed. Some days I felt were harder than others, and some obstacles seemed so impossible to overcome, but to God be the glory! With gratitude and faith, all things are possible. And every day is a new chance to be grateful.

This memoir came from much reflection on God's love, living under God's rules in His Boot Camp.

Earlier I told you, my reader, how I met Greenbrier. He is a psychiatrist but not my psychiatrist. I told him not to analyze me! He did, however, teach me to have a lifestyle that I call "being present." I told him about my past when he wanted to marry me.

When my children were three and four years old, I was already in our big house that God gave us. We didn't have all the things we have been blessed to have now. We lived in an empty house. We said we would not go into credit card debt but rather would pray God to "give us this day our daily bread." When God could trust us with stuff, He would provide. We have since been richly blessed by Him.

The concept of "rethinking obstacles" has let me thank God in everything. Prejudice is just one obstacle but a good example of a principle I wish to teach. Many years ago I was so upset from not having any close friends. I felt discriminated against. That's exactly how I felt. I know what discrimination is all about. Before I never knew what discrimination was about, because no one discriminated against me in the Philippines. I was treated well. But I came to America and I really felt bad.

I'm older now, I'm 73. Imagine all these years. I came in 1970. It's over 40 years in the wilderness of the United States of America. I never told my parents about my troubles, about my time in the cuckoo's nest, because I didn't want them to worry. The last time when they came here to visit, my father said, "It's the land of the free and home of the brave."

I just kept quiet. I couldn't tell them, "I came here to be free and I lost my freedom in the United States." I lost my freedom in America, in the land of the free.

God provided a way around my obstacle when I became the doctor for our true American heroes—our Veterans. They freed my homeland from Japanese oppression in WWII. And if they had not fought so hard, it may have been that we here in America would all be speaking German or Japanese today. Now I have had a life where I can say my American patients, families, and the health care team with whom I closely worked love me! I feel no discrimination. I see no obstacles.

Finally, with the heart I remember to be wowed!

IF CHRIST TARRIES

Pastor Robert K. Spradling of Charleston Bible Center Church, who married Greenbrier and me on Saturday, September 13, 1975, used to pepper his conversation with the phrase "if Christ tarries." I have lived nearly 74 years expecting any day to see Christ returning. Nothing would please me more.

However, today I write this memoir figuring God's direction "to write it (my story) down" is a significant order. I write of feelings experienced along this way of life.

My mother is buried in West Virginia, along with my father. When my family comes to visit I will give them my book. They will learn more than I have ever said before.

When Greenbrier asked me to write, I resisted because I didn't want to write the book. Over time I have told my friends Judy and Linda parts only, but I never told them all. I thought I should tell my friends about it even though I have some anxiety in the telling. So I told them my own feelings. I love America. I came because I love America. But I think I was treated as an enemy. That's exactly how I feel. I was treated as an enemy, but that is not who I am.

But through it all, I became closer to God. I am thanking people who gave me a hard time now because, as a result of that, many things happened. I could have been hurt, but God protected me.

The last time I was in a Charismatic group was in the Philippines. The Methodists don't worship with charismatic gifts evident. They believe in the Holy Spirit, but the Charismatic group is more into that kind of thing. The Foursquare Gospel Church (in the Philippines) is like that. An Assembly of God pastor named Shane Cunningham was visiting from Australia. He was invited to speak in the church. I went there alone, because my sisters didn't want to go there on a Sunday night. I was going back to the United States soon. So I went to church alone. I walked maybe one mile and attended church. I was sitting in the second row, nobody else was sitting in my row. No one was in the front row. (Nobody sits in the front row in church, even in the Philippines!) So I was close to the podium. The pastor came and he began praying. He wasn't preaching. He started praying for healing for people. I just watched the people around me as a spectator. I got bored after a while, because he was just praying, not preaching. Then I saw people in the third row at the very end, the opposite end from the podium, whom I knew, so I went to talk to them. I didn't know their names but I knew their faces because they grew up with me. So I went to them. Suddenly this pastor was in front of me.

Let me say, I was surprised. I thought he was praying for the sick people, but suddenly he was in front of me. He said, "I see faces. Not just a few faces, but a lot of faces." That's what he said. "God is going to use you. It will be like bowling," he said. "It will be easy for you."

I said, "Easy?"

"Yes, it will be easy, because you are not the one to be doing it. It will be God doing it."

That was in 2014. "If Christ tarries," I will understand more. I don't know. He said it will be easy for me. But I don't know what to do. I'm just an ordinary person. He said it will be easy because God will be the one doing it. So what could I say? "Praise the Lord," that's all I could say. Then he left and preached his sermon. But after some time I would think about that, what it all meant in my life.

My parents honored me by putting their bodies here. So we bought 16 graves. I will be buried here in West Virginia, too, "if Christ tarries." Even if I die in the Philippines, I think I would like for my body to be brought here. I am a West Virginian. I have lived in America longer than I have lived in the Philippines. (I was only 28 years old when I came to America.) We shall see how my life ends and what else God has in store for me to do, "if Christ tarries."

GOOD COURAGE

One of my lessons learned in coming to America was to be of "good courage." I missed my parents and the cultural nest of the Philippines. Unbeknownst to me at that time, I was enlisted in God's Boot Camp. I figured out how to have a much richer life!

> Be ye free from the love of money; content with such things as ye have: for himself hath said, I will in no wise fail thee, neither will I in any wise forsake thee. So that with good courage we say, The Lord is my helper; I will not fear: What shall man do unto me?
>
> —Hebrews 13:5-6

God had blessed me with musical talent which I have developed for His glory. Our home church has Lenten/Easter luncheons. One time the leaders asked me to sing. I selected "His Eye Is on the Sparrow." Before I sang, I testified. Exalting God elevated me. What came out from my soul was special. I was inspired. Something was in my brain dictating what I should say. Though I scarcely recall, I remember that I said something about the year 1972, relating a story about being lost in the United States. Then I sang the song.

One woman there, a minister named Marianna Harr, cried with emotion. Afterward she told me that I was beautiful inside and out. Her own tears flowed freely. She cried loudly while I was singing that song. Usually in mainline Protestant churches the worship is not this Spirit-filled. After seeing Rev. Harr's tears and receiving her "thanks-giving" offering, I didn't say anything, because what could I say? "You are beautiful inside and out." From then on until her death, she would say that every Sunday in church. She sat in the pew behind us at FUMC.

And one man, I don't know who he was, came to me after my singing and said, "That's the most perfect speech I have ever heard." Let me hasten to say, my speech was not mine. My soul expressed it.

What I believe happened that day has parallels in the Bible. There it is written not to worry about what you will speak because God will give you words. I have experienced that. How refreshing! The Bible is inspired writing using inspired men. They wrote because God told them what to write. When that happened to me at that time, wow! It was not my speech but was God-inspired.

When I look back on my life now, I am amazed. "It's amazing grace," I cried when I realized. "How sweet the sound that saved a wretch like me." It's true, because He saved my life. I could have been dead, gone forever.

Greenbrier and I visited St. Kitts Island in the Caribbean. There we learned John Newton, a slave ship captain, had a life-changing experience, penning "Amazing Grace." Standing there looking at those sugar cane fields previously tended by African slaves, we marveled that all the slaves are freed and the island now houses two medical schools and a veterinarian school. God's higher purpose is evident in that land of the blue skies, blue waters and warm temperatures.

I can now pray for such blessings for my Philippine Islands.

Making it through God's Boot Camp, I have faith to see that when Jesus said, "Take my yoke," He was making a way to serve God that for me, a little island girl, would be impossible but with God's help is easy.

"Easy?"

"Yes, it will be easy, because God will be doing it."

This was the message from a Charismatic Word of Knowledge a few years ago (2014). The Evangelist didn't know me; he is from Australia. It's amazing.

Now I see God's "good courage" sufficient day by day.

HIDDEN TREASURE

> If thou seekest her as silver, and searchest for her as for hid treasures; Then shalt thou understand the fear of the Lord, and find the knowledge of God.
>
> —Proverbs 2:4-5

Christ is coming back soon. I don't know when. Maybe in my lifetime. Who knows? When I was maybe 11 or 12 years old, I dreamt almost every night about the coming of Jesus Christ. I wonder why. But I always dreamt about it when I was about that age.

Now I am 73. I told God, "If You're going to use me, use me now. I am getting old, I may be weak soon."

My mind said, "God called Moses when he was 80." There you have it. I may live to be 100. Of course my life belongs to God, it is not mine anymore. I don't own anything, I don't even own my life anymore. I think God has allowed me the process of being in His Boot Camp to learn many things about Him. He is true. He is real.

You can see that in my life too, that God is with me. And it might not be right now, because God's day is 1000 years, and 1000 years is a day to Him. And His ways are not our ways.

God's ways are to be searched for like a hidden treasure. When I grew up in the Filipino Catholic culture, I saw life from that perspective. I had glimpses of Heaven but I misunderstood clues that God gave. I used to be very narrow-minded. I used to say, "Oh, those Catholics. Catholics don't really know anything, they are not Christians." But God showed me I have no right to say that, because some Catholics are better than Protestants in their lifestyle. Only God will judge anyway. They are the same, they are Christians too. They believe in Christ. They are not the enemy.

When I came to America, I was risking being in a golden cage in the richest country in the world. I thought maybe the title of my book would be *The Golden Cage*, but God thought differently.

God thought differently about other things as well. I had already passed by medical test. "I am a doctor," I thought. "I am self-sufficient, I can do it." That's what I said to myself when I turned down my suitor. I thought, "Well, I'm a doctor. I can work hard. I won't be poor." But God took it away from me. I landed in the cuckoo's nest, I lost my residency, I did not pass my Pediatric certification boards. But in His goodness He didn't take my license away from me. He allowed me to work. But I had to learn to rely on Him and His grace, not just to rely on myself. Here I am just a pilgrim passing through. This world is not my home. My eternal home has no curse. No more curse and no more darkness. Our eternal home will clearly be a marvelous place!

I actually don't have bitter feelings about the people who hurt me. I think God is in there, so do I hate God? God has reasons for it, why He allowed it. He allowed all those things. I don't hate anybody even now. I don't know why I don't have that kind of feeling, but I don't. I would say, "It's not me you have to ask forgiveness from. Go to God, not me."

That's my life. All by God's grace I am here. And God has been good to me.

Everything is in God's direction. I have come to a point in my life that I can see my nothingness, my self-sufficiency. I just tell my friend Linda, "I am here. I went through boot camp, God's Boot Camp. Now I am in the army. I am a private."

Somebody said, "Oh, you should be an officer." Maybe God will raise me up or promote me. But right now I am just a private.

When I came back from my medical mission in Central

America, I thought, "What is God trying to do to me?" I had lost my residency. I was looking for His will, His direction. I picked up a tract in 1972 and stapled it in my Bible. It read:

> And thine ears shall hear a word behind thee, saying, This is the way, walk ye in it, when ye turn to the right hand, and when ye turn to the left.
>
> —Isaiah 30:21

and

> I will instruct thee and teach thee in the way which thou shalt go: I will guide thee with mine eye.
>
> —Psalm 32:8

God has kept His promise to me, and has led me to hidden treasure beyond my wildest dreams.

AFTERWORD

I belong to Jesus, my God and Lord. It took a lifetime of God's training in His Boot Camp.

I know now from following Jesus and being His disciple that He asks for our obedience to His wishes. Obey, obey, obey. Then you can walk with God.

Does anyone want to know God? Obey His commands. He asks for total obedience, but what a thrill it is to know He cares for every detail of our lives. He is faithful, full of love and mercy. He is Sovereign.

Believe in the Lord Jesus and have life eternal with God. We are souls that live eternally. We are in a body that enjoys earth for a short time. We are given a choice while on earth to believe that Jesus is who He claims He is—God who loves us and died for us. Jesus is Savior and Lord of all. Anyone who believes has eternal life with God; all glory be His!

ALSO AVAILABLE

Harold D. Almond, MD:
The Stories of a West Virginia Doctor

Stories of Harold Almond, MD as told to
Greenbrier Almond, MD:
*Tender Loving Care: Stories of a West Virginia Doctor,
Volume Two*

Greenbrier Almond, MD:
Stories of a West Virginia Doctor's Son

*Stories of a West Virginia Doctor for His
Grandchildren*

Stories of a West Virginia Doctor for Kith and Kin

Greenbrier Almond, K Almond, Anne Almond,
Ruthie Almond Wiewiora, Beth Almond Ford:
Stories of a West Virginia Family

Available from:
McClain Printing Company
1-800-654-7179   www.mcclainprinting.com

West Virginia Book Company
1-888-982-7472   www.wvbookco.com

Amazon.com   Barnesandnoble.com

Artistry on Main
27 E. Main St. Buckhannon, WV 26201

Upshur County Historical Society
29 and 81 W. Main St. Buckhannon, WV 26201